DRAMA THROUGH THE CHURCH YEAR

by
JUDY GATTIS SMITH

MERIWETHER PUBLISHING LTD.
Colorado Springs, Colorado

Meriwether Publishing Ltd., Publisher
P.O. Box 7710
Colorado Springs, CO 80933

typography by Shirley Heath
edited by Arthur Zapel
cover design by Michelle Zapel

ISBN: 0-916260-26-7
© Copyright MCMLXXXIV
Meriwether Publishing Ltd.
printed in the United States of America
First Edition
Library of Congress # 84-61476

To Mother —
who lives very close to the seasons
and who first fostered my love
for drama and for the Church

TABLE OF CONTENTS

INTRODUCTION

The dramatic impulse is as old as man. There is evidence of an Abydos Passion play in Egypt perhaps 5,000 years ago. Drama originated in religious dances and ceremonies. The history of drama and religion has waxed and waned and expressed itself in sometimes powerful and bizarre ways. But, even though it has gone through periods of ill favor in the church, drama continually rises like a phoenix force from the ashes. There is something deep within a human being that finds expression through drama.

The phony, the artificial, the make believe portrays a greater truth. It touches deep notes in our lives. It gives expression to inner feelings. We use make believe to bring to the fore our inner yearnings.

This book attempts to contain this "phoenix" force within the confines of a local church and to harness dramatic expression to the ebb and flow of the Liturgical Year. It focuses on the seasons of the church year and the seasons of the calendar. What is the appeal of a particular month? Within the framework of both Liturgical and Seasonal considerations this book offers suggestions for dramatic methods and ideas that seem appropriate.

Drama in the church finds voice in three areas:

1. Education
2. Recreation
3. Worship

This book is designed to assist persons interested in starting a local church drama program or revitalizing an already existing program. It is for persons who need ideas. It can assist directors of church drama groups in the selection of plays suitable for production in keeping with the feelings of the church year. This book offers ideas that have been tried on a local level and suggests resources that are available from Contemporary Drama Service.

The plays noted within are only suggestions. They will give you an idea of similar plays you may write yourself or purchase from other sources. It is my purpose in this book to demonstrate possibilities only — to stimulate your creative mind while saving you many hours of preliminary planning.

As an example, we have a PAS-time program (as suggested in September Chapter) at the Williamsburg United Methodist Church where I worship and serve. When I gave some resources to a new leader recently, she said "Thank you. You have done the spade work, now I can adapt it myself and concentrate on the children."

Come take an imaginary trip with me — through a church — your church alive with drama. Walk through the corridors of the Church School. Peep into rooms and see small children pantomiming and acting with the movements of their bodies. See older children simply costumed, acting out a Bible story. See teenagers role playing a situation from their daily lives. See Adult Church School classes listening to a play reading. See the intensity. Feel the excitement. Notice the potential being released from the actors — the learning taking place. Sense the freedom, the spontaneity, the creativity, the fun.

Now move into the Fellowship Hall. See a structured drama being presented by the persons from your church. See the discipline of a group that subjects individual freedom and creativity to cooperation and sensitivity to others for the purpose of proclaiming the glory of God. See the theatre picture unfolding before the audience. See the actors (your fellow churchmen) subjecting their own feelings and problems to the integrity of the play.

Let's continue our imaginary journey. See your congregation in a fellowship setting. See persons opening up to others through theatre games. Hear the laughter. Feel the warmth. Notice the ease of sharing through the vehicle of skits and games. Feel the deepening of fellowship.

See persons from your church moving out into the streets, the community as clowns, as parades. Going forth joyfully with exaggerated costumes and wild props and moving sets. Join the parade for a moment. March with your fellow churchmen. Get caught up in the festivities.

Now move into your Sanctuary. In this awe-filled holy setting watch a lived moment from our heritage unfold. Join in acted motions that have brought us to God throughout the years. Feel the great worship themes — thanksgiving, praise, forgiveness, hope, dedication — reverently and beautifully portrayed.

Do you like this image of your church? It can be yours. Whether small church or large, your people can know the joy of being involved in dramatic activity. There is no better way to break down the barriers of loneliness, shyness or a narrow routing. It is within the reach of every church. It is yours to grasp if only you will.

How do we begin to bring this image to life?

There must be a core of interested persons. Although from the beginning you want to foster the idea that drama is inclusive, not exclusive. Still there must be the "few" who band together to start your plan and bring reality to your dream.

The fun and excitement of drama in a local church is that this core group does not have to be made up of professionals. Stage-struck teenagers, creative Church School teachers, sensitive worship planners, uninhibited, artistic individuals, retired persons with newly found time on their hands — all can come together under the umbrella of "Local Church Drama" and create a program for your church that is vital, alive and exciting.

So your first step is to sniff out these individuals. There may be as few as three or four to begin. Get a cup of coffee, sit around a table, hash out some of the ideas in this book. Decide if you want to begin such an experience of drama in your local church.

In many churches your next step would be to bring the idea to the planning body of your church. Planning is a means to get what you want. Remember our Biblical heritage. In Genesis 41, Joseph created a fourteen year plan to deal with famine.

Working within your local church framework broadens your base of support. It gets your idea woven into the whole fabric of the church's life. It integrates drama into the church's total program. Come before this group with a dream and a plan. Infuse them with some of your small group's enthusiasm.

What do you need in the way of support? At first just the permission to go ahead. Ideally sponsors will bring to the project financial support and serve as publicity agents later. Sponsors need to be educated and it is well to list what is needed. Announce a project on a modest scale and you will get a modest response. So share your big dream.

Now with the approval of your church planning group your next step is to reach out in a broader, more inclusive manner. Create a drama calendar for the year for your church as a framework in which to function. In many cases the rhythm and flow of the Liturgical Year dictates the type of drama on which you will be working. For example September and the beginning of school seem a natural time to begin drama in the Church School, November suggests pageantry and processions and December, chancel drama.

Following is a suggested calendar but feel free to change it and work within the structure of your church.

A drama activity is suggested for every month but this will probably be too much for one drama group within one year. Pick and choose for your local needs.

This book begins in September because it is a time of year when the lethargy of the Summer drops from us and families fall into more structured routines. We are open to new ideas and new beginnings. We feel we could run up a mountain and then run back.

DRAMA CALENDAR

SEPT

Beginning;
Workshop for Teachers
Ongoing;
Dramatic Activity
for Children

OCT

Family Night of Fun,
Youth Play &
Drama Games

NOV

Parades, Processionals,
Pageantry &
Choral Reading

DEC

Chancel
Drama

JAN

Play Reading,
Writing Historical Dramas

FEB

An All-Church Revue —
Acts, Skits & Dramas

MAR

Intergenerational
Study of Lent & Easter
Through Drama

APR

Movement &
Liturgical Dance

MAY

One-Act Plays,
Monologues &
Spontaneous Drama

JUN

Drama Moves into
the Community;
Puppets, Clowns
& Parades

JUL

Accoutrements of
Drama Workshop;
Make-up, Scenery
& Costumes

AUG

Drama Games
& Stories

INDEX OF WHERE DRAMA TAKES PLACE

SEPTEMBER:

Drama Workshop for Church School Teachers, PAS-time Program

September is here! We have the approval of the Church Planning Body. Let's go! Your first impulse may be to begin with a dramatic production. These core persons, interested in drama are ready to put on a play. If this works best in your situation a production can be a good kick-off for drama in your church. However, let me encourage you to take a longer range view. Experience teaches that in many places it is hard to get persons together in summer for rehearsals and sometimes putting on one play dampens the fuse of the drama group. All their energies go into this production, the group becomes "select" and we lose the larger vision of drama as a permeating force throughout the entire church.

Rather, follow these directions for September:

1. Make your Church School teachers aware of drama as a potential for teaching. Have an all-day workshop for teachers. Introduce drama in the Church School classroom on all age levels. Following this, representatives from the core group lead informal drama in the classrooms or help the Church School teachers lead drama.

2. Begin a weekly, on-going program for children utilizing drama.

DRAMA WORKSHOP FOR TEACHERS

For: Church School teachers of all age levels (four years and above) in the church.

Meeting Room: Large area like a Fellowship Hall with movable chairs arranged in semi-circle with stage area.

Introduction: Drama and Christian Education have a lot in common. Both seek to release the potential within each participating individual.

Everyone is familiar with such phrases as "learning by doing". We have heard the Chinese proverb which says:

I hear and I forget, I see and I remember, I do and I understand.

Drama capitalizes on these insights.

Drama also has the characteristic of making Sunday School fun for children. Sunday School becomes a welcome opportunity rather than a duty.

The teacher is the initial source of interest and enthusiasm for drama. If the teacher approaches drama with a sense of joy, the children will pick it up. They will carry it through their lives and want to pass it on to their children. It is an invaluable gift for life.

Teachers should always keep in mind that drama in the Church School classroom places emphasis on subject rather than the techniques of production.

LEADER: We act in two ways — speech and movement of the human body.

Movement: Let's start with movement. As adults we get so use to words, floods of words, that we forget that other things can tell us a great deal — a movement of the hand or foot or even a finger can communicate a message to us.

In the midst of a sea of words we sometimes forget the one means of communication that is more effective, that "speaks" anywhere in the world, and is timeless. This wordless communication is pantomime. It is as old as man and as modern as television and we use it all the time.

To loosen us up and show you that everyone can act let's play a game. I'll give each of you an instruction. Will you then stand up and show the group how to do what I ask with pantomime?

1.   Say with your palm "Stop" *(palm up and outward).*

2.   Say with your head "Yes" *(nod head)*, and so on around the room.

3. Say with your eyes "I don't understand" *(raised eyebrows, blink eyes in amazement)*.

4. Say with your foot "I'm waiting".
   Leader: This one is interesting because invariably children and adults respond to this differently. Children stand on one foot, the other foot rubbing behind their leg. Adults pat their foot impatiently.

5. Say with your ear "I hear the phone ringing" *(tilt ear upward and look up sideways)*.

6. Say with your tongue *(no words)* "I like chocolate cake" *(roll tongue around lips)*.

7. Say with your finger "Come here" *(beckon coyly with finger)*.

8. Say with fingertip "I touched a hot stove" *(touch imaginary spot, then jerk away)*.

9. Say with your nose "I smell popcorn" *(sniff in appreciation)*.

You can think of others to add until every teacher has had an opportunity to respond.

LEADER: Now, how can we carry this over into the Church School?

In working with children pantomime is perhaps more important, certainly more underlying, than speech. First pantomimes of children are imitative. They do what they see others do. Before four years, drama is really just play but at four most children can respond to an echo pantomime. In an echo pantomime the teacher tells a story with words and actions and children repeat their teacher's action. As an example, the following excerpt from the children's play A Journey With Jesus Through Holy Week, *Palm Sunday,* by Judy Gattis Smith, published by Contemporary Drama Service.

WORDS	ACTIONS
I was a child in Jesus' day.	*(Stand straight and smile)*
One day I put on my sandals. . .	*(Slip on sandals)*
And put on my robe	*(Slip arms into cloak)*
And hurried to the city gate.	*(Run in place)*

WORDS (contd)	ACTIONS
I was very happy and excited.	*(Big smile)*
I called my friends to join me	*(Beckon with arm)*
And told them that Jesus was this way.	*(Talk to each other)*
We walked on together.	*(Walk in place)*
Some of my friends were already there.	*(Wave greeting)*
We were all so excited.	*(Jump up and down)*
We looked to see if he was coming	*(Shade eyes)*
But we saw nothing.	*(Shake head "no")*
It was hard for us to wait.	*(Shift from one foot to another)*
Then we saw a tiny figure in the distance.	*(Point ahead)*
Could it be Jesus?	*(Hands ask question)*
We left our parents and ran ahead.	*(Run in place)*
Yes, it was Jesus and he was coming our way	*(Stop running and point)*
He was riding a donkey and his disciples walked behind.	*(Slap one thigh, then the other, then clap hands, repeat)*

Movement can be used in other ways to get children into a story. As an example, the following excerpt from the children's play Tell Me Some Stories About Jesus, *The Storm At Sea*, by Judy Gattis Smith, published by Contemporary Drama Service.

THE STORM AT SEA
Luke 4:35-41

Have you ever been caught in a sudden storm? Have you ever seen a storm at sea? Once Jesus was in a terrible tempest on the Sea of Galilee.

To help us better understand this story, I want you all to help me by making sound effects. We'll divide into three groups.

Group 1 — Waves — start gently, swishing hands together — become louder by slapping hands together and then become ferocious by making your hands into fists and pounding desks, or tables, or pews.

Group 2 — Wind — start blowing gently and slowly just letting air escape between your lips, then puff air quickly and finally then make loud whistling sound.

Group 3 — Boat Rocking — side-to-side first gently and slowly, then wilder and faster.

It was almost twilight when Jesus and the disciples stepped into the small boat to row across the Sea of Galilee to the other side.

A gentle wind was blowing. *(Sound — Group 2)*

And waves were lapping against the boat's side. *(Hands rub together to form swishing sound, Group 1)*

The boat slid smoothly through the water. *(Group 3 sways gently)*

Jesus, tired from his labors of the day, lay down in the back of the boat and was soon asleep.

Bending their backs, rowing in rhythm, the disciples pulled the oars through the water. *(Groups 1, 2, and 3 — gentle sounds)*

When the boat was far from shore the sky began to glow with an eerie light.

The wind began to blow faster. *(Puffing sound — Group 2)*

The waves began to get higher and slap against the sides. *(Slap hands together at least 6 claps — Group 1)*

The clouds began to grow darker. One of the sudden storms common to the Sea of Galilee was approaching rapidly.

The small boat began to rock. *(Rock back and forth — Group 3)*

The waves angrily pounded the boat. *(Hands make fists and pound, Group 1)*

Now the wind was roaring. *(Whistling sound — Group 2)*

The disciples pulled the oars with all their strength but the great waves dashed their ship helplessly about. *(Swaying — Group 3)*

Far from shore in the fury of the storm, the disciples feared they might never see land again. *(Sounds — Groups 1, 2 and 3)*

Several of the disciples had seen the rage of the sea at other times when storms swept over its surface. They knew the fearful power of such a storm. They knew how helpless they were in the grasp of this tempest. While they were wondering what to do, a great wave broke over the side of the ship, flooding it with water. Now they believed they would all be drowned.

Then they remembered Jesus asleep in the boat.

Everyone, help me call Jesus:

(Audience: "Wake up! Wake up! Don't you care that we are about to die?")

Jesus woke from his sleep and saw their alarm.

He listened to the wind blowing fiercely. *(Sound — Group 2)*

And he said, "Be quiet." And the winds were silent. He listened to the waves pound furiously. *(Sound — Group 1)* And he said, "Be still." And there was a great calm on the water.

He saw the little boat rocking dangerously. *(Group 3)* And he commanded it to be steady. At the sound of his voice, the terrible tempest dissolved.

The waves lapped gently. *(Hands swish — Group 1)*

The wind blew a soothing breeze. *(Sound — Group 2)*

The boat bobbed peacefully *(Gentle swaying — Group 3)* and he turned to his disciples and asked, "Why are you so frightened? Do you still have no faith?"

Then the disciples were filled with awe and fear and they said to one another, "Who is this man? Even the wind and the waves obey him."

Even adults can become more involved in a Bible story by using their bodies. Following is a parable which involves adults in a non-threatening way.

"Once Peter, the great disciple of Jesus, tried to bargain with God. He said to Jesus, 'Master, we have given up everything to follow you — our homes, our families, our friends, our work, everything. What reward will God give us? How will he repay our goodness?'

In answer to his questions Jesus told a story, a story about some workers in a vineyard. Will you help me tell that story now?

Once a man owned a very fine vineyard that gave a wonderful harvest of grapes. Grape harvest came in August or September just before the rainy season began. One day the farmer noticed the first grapes were beginning to get ripe. *(Will the front rows on my Left stand up and be the grapes growing?)*

Then more grapes ripened. *(Next two rows on Left stand up. Leader encourages them to take shape of grapevines.)*

The farmer realized that all his grapes were getting ripe at the same time. *(Everyone on Left stand up)* You are the grape harvest. This is the finest harvest of grapes that the farmer has ever had. Vines were weighed down to the ground by great bunches of fat, juicy grapes. *(Leader encourages group to make creative responses)*

This harvest has to be gathered quickly before the heavy rains come or the farmer will lose his entire crop.

The farmer needed a great many workers to pick the grapes, so he went into town to hire men from those who waited in the market-place for any work that was to be had. The farmer went right at sun-rise. The best workers were already there. These were good workmen who were ready to bargain for the best wages they could get for a day's work. Day's work began at sunup and went until sundown. The farmer was a fair and just man, so he offered a denarius to the man for a full day's work. This was a generous offer. It was a good day's pay for a laborer. The men agreed to go and they set off for the farm. *(Will the last two rows on the Right please stand up? You are the good laborers who agree on the full day's work. How can you show us that you are the best workers? You see those grapes over there? Indicate Left. You are going to have to work very hard to gather all those fat bunches of grapes in your baskets.)*

The farmer checked the fields about nine o'clock. Only a portion of the grapes had been gathered. *(One row on the Left or half a row can sit down to indicate grapes picked)*

So the farmer went back to the marketplace again looking for more men to work. He found some and hired them at once. *(Two more rows on Right Back stand up)* You are the pretty good workers who started at nine o'clock.

Later the farmer checked the vineyards again. All the men were working well, but still only a small portion of the grapes had been picked. *(Few more on the Left sit down, as indicated by Leader.)* You have been picked.

Again the farmer went to the marketplace. It was nearly midday, but there were still men there waiting for work. *(Some men on the Right stand up)* These were also hired for work. They helped a great deal but still only a portion of the grapes were picked. *(More on the Left sit down)*

It went on like this all day. The farmer had to hire more men in the afternoon. *(Others on the Right stand up as hired workers)* Now the vineyard was buzzing with busy workers, gathering grapes as fast as they could. *(Few more on the Left sit down)* But still there were a lot more bunches to be picked.

Now it was almost five o'clock. There was only an hour left for work before sundown. The farmer went again to the marketplace, for every minute mattered. He was surprised to find some men lolling there. They were the men that no one would hire. Times were bad and even good workers were often out of work. These men were not very strong and could not work very hard. They seldom got any work at all. They too, had wives and children to feed and to clothe. The farmer felt sorry for them and sent them to the vineyard. *(Remainder of persons on the Right stand up)* At six o'clock the long day's work ended. All the grapes had been picked and the harvest was saved. *(All the remainder of grapes on the Left sit down)*

Now the farmer came out of the house and lined the laborers up for their wages.

First he paid those who were hired last — one denarius apiece. *(These workers sit)*

Then he paid those hired at noonday — one denarius. *(They may sit)*

Next he paid those hired during the morning — one denarius. *(They may sit)*

Finally he paid those who had worked from sunup to sundown — one denarius. You have been standing a long time. How do you feel about this? Do you think it is fair?

Neither did those workers. They became very angry.

The farmer asked, "Why are you angry?" What would you have said *(To workers left standing on Right)*?

The laborers shouted, "We want a fair wage. We've slaved all day in your vineyard. We've sweated through the heat of the sun for twelve solid hours and you gave us the same pay as those lay-abouts who've only done one hour's work. We want our rights!"

The farmer answered, "You seem to think I have cheated you. I have done no wrong. Didn't you agree with me to do a day's work for one silver denarius? That is exactly what I paid you. You kept your part of the agreement. I have kept mine. This was our bargain. What are you grumbling about? Because I paid all the other men the same as you? But that's my business, not yours. Can't I do what I like with my own money? Why should you complain just because I choose to be generous?Are you full of envy, just because I was kind to the other workers? You have gotten exactly what you bargained for. *(Remaining workers sit)*

This was a strange story for Jesus to tell, wasn't it? It turned everything upside-down. God is like the farmer. He loves to be generous. Those who bargain with him get only what they bargain for. Those who simply trust in him receive far more than they could ever deserve or expect. Those who expect nothing receive more than they could ever dream of.

This was Peter's answer. It is foolish to think we can bargain with God. We can only trust in him and rely on his goodness and generosity."*

Speech: Sometimes we work in crowded spaces and can't get up and act. Our second method of acting is speech. People have become so accustomed to formal or produced plays that the idea of reading may seem dull and uninteresting. Experience will be the only convincer. Words alone can be a form of drama as in a choral reading. (More on choral reading in November chapter.)

As an example, the following excerpt (See pgs. 12 and 13) from the children's play Four Parables Of Jesus, *The Lost Son*, by Judy Gattis Smith, published by Contemporary Drama Service.

*From Come Children, Praise & Pray, Copyright 1977, C.S.S. Publishing Company, Inc., Lima, Ohio. Used with permission.

CHORUS I:	"The Lost Son"
CHORUS II:	A parable told by Jesus
CHORUS I:	Many years ago there lived a man who had two sons
CHORUS II:	The oldest son was dependable
CHORUS I:	Steady and hard-working
CHORUS II:	Reliable and honest
CHORUS I:	A model son
CHORUS II:	But the younger son was happy-go-lucky
CHORUS I:	Thoughtless and impulsive
CHORUS II:	Unreliable
CHORUS I:	They were living well enough together until one day the younger son thought:
YOUNG. SON:	Why am I wasting all my youth living here with my father? I want to see things and go places and do things.
CHORUS II:	*(Whisper)* Run away, run away. Take your inheritance and run away.
YOUNG. SON:	Did someone say "run away?"
CHORUS II:	*(Louder)* Run away, run away. Take your inheritance and run away.
YOUNG. SON:	That's a wonderful idea. That's exactly what I'll do.
CHORUS I:	And that's exactly what he did. He went to his Father and said:
YOUNG. SON:	Father, give me now my share of the property so that I can see things and go places and do things.
CHORUS II:	So the father divided the property between his two sons.
CHORUS I:	And the older son who was steady and hard-working
CHORUS II:	Reliable and honest
CHORUS I:	A model son — stayed at home
CHORUS II:	And the younger son who was happy-go-lucky
CHORUS I:	Thoughtless and impulsive
CHORUS II:	Sold his part of the property and left home with his money
CHORUS I:	He took his money and went away
CHORUS II:	Skipping and running
CHORUS I:	Whistling and laughing
CHORUS II:	He took his money and went away
CHORUS I:	*(Whisper)* Spend your money, spend your money Live it up and spend your money
YOUNG. SON:	Did someone say spend my money?
CHORUS I:	*(Louder)* It's only money. Spend it, spend it. Live it up and spend your money
YOUNG. SON:	That's a wonderful idea. That's exactly what I'll do
CHORUS II:	And that's exactly what he did
CHORUS I:	And he saw all the things he wanted to see
CHORUS II:	And he went all the places he wanted to go.
CHORUS I:	And he did all the things he wanted to do

	"The Lost Son" *(contd)*
CHORUS II:	*(Slower)* But one day he woke up and found himself in a far away country
CHORUS I:	And he had no friends
CHORUS II:	And he had no house
CHORUS I:	And he had no money
CHORUS II:	And a famine was sweeping the land
CHORUS I:	What will he do? What will he do?
CHORUS II:	Where can he go? What will he eat?
CHORUS I:	*(Whisper)* Find a job. Find a job. You are going to starve. Find a job.
YOUNG. SON:	Did someone say find a job?
CHORUS I:	*(Louder)* Find a job. Find a job. You are going to starve. Find a job.
YOUNG. SON:	That's a wonderful idea. That's exactly what I'll do.
CHORUS II:	And that's exactly what he did. He went to live with one of the citizens of that country.

Reader's Theatre is a method that uses words to teach adults. (More information on Reader's Theatre is found in January chapter.) An example of this is the following excerpt from the play The Problem Of World Hunger, by Peg Oliver, published by Contemporary Drama Service.

THE PROBLEM OF WORLD HUNGER

(All characters can speak from the front, or First Christian can be in the pulpit; American Christian can speak from the congregation, on the American side; Third World Voices can speak from the "Hungry" part of the congregation. All will stand for their lines and dialogues, talking to each other. Third World Speakers can wear shawls or turban-like head-dresses.)

FIRST WORLD	
CHRISTIAN:	460 million people in the world are acutely hungry.
AMER. CHRIS.:	What do you really mean when you say hunger? I mean, I think I know . . .
VOICE 1:	Hunger is a child with shriveled limbs and a swollen belly.
VOICE 2:	Hunger is the grief of parents or a person gone blind for lack of Vitamin A.
VOICE 1:	The body consumes itself and deteriorates rapidly.
VOICE 2:	Confusion sets in; starvation affects the mind.

VOICE 1:	In the next minute, 28 of us will die from starvation.
VOICE 2:	Most will be children.
AMER. CHRIS.:	You mean all those people — how many were there?
FIRST W.C.:	460 million who are victims of acute hunger. More than 1 billion are severely undernourished.
AMER. CHRIS.:	All those people — it's just too much for me to visualize.
FIRST W.C.:	*(Divides up the congregation)* Altogether, you're the 4 billion people in the world. On the right, you're well or adequately fed. The left half is undernourished, acutely hungry, or starving.
AMER. CHRIS:	Well, I feel terrible about that, of course, but there's nothing anyone can do, is there? There's no possible way that enough food could be produced for all those people.
VOICE 1:	Enough food is produced every day for every man, woman, and child on earth.
VOICE 2:	There is no country in this world where the people could not feed themselves from their own resources.
AMER. CHRIS.:	Then why can't they all feed themselves? Why are they hungry?
FIRST W.C.:	What do you think is the problem?
AMER. CHRIS.:	Well, it's always seemed to me that overpopulation is the problem. *(To the Third World People)* Why don't you stop having so many babies? Why won't you accept birth control? It's for your own good!

Break: Chance to stretch, get a drink, look over material.

When we combine the two methods of acting, speech and movement, we have the most common form of drama used in the Church school: role playing. In role playing the characters and general situation are given, but students make up action and dialogue from their own imaginations . . .

The Bible is full of characters who flash for a moment on the screen and are gone. We get only brief glimpses of persons whose lives momentarily cross paths with Jesus or other central Biblical figures and then we hear no more of them: the boy with the loaves and fishes, the rich young ruler, Barabas, the Christmas shepherds. As we read of these people haunting questions arise — What happened next? Where were they ten years later? How much of an impact did this brief encounter cause in their lives?

We can find one answer to these questions by looking into our own experiences. We can vicariously put ourselves into that Biblical lived moment and draw upon what we know of human experience and encounter. Through role play we do just this. Unlike much role play used in our Church School our role play will not be completely spontaneous but will be performed in the framework of structured scenes.

1. First read the situation as it appears in the Bible.

2. Read background material that might prove helpful.

3. Most important step — Cast of Characters. For your scene there should be one main character, two or more supporting characters and an antagonist. The teacher asks questions to talk the students into the roles, to make the characters three dimensional, to help the students become that person, and to help others in the scene also see the person. Do not force persons against their will to participate. Assume persons will participate.

4. Briefly act out scene.

5. Discuss reactions and feelings. Were the characters believable? Is this an honest portrayal? Is it a believable answer to the question of "What happened next?"

6. After analyzing do the scene again or do a scene of the characters ten years later. Role play is often more useful the third and fourth time around in a given scene. By this time some of the awkwardness is over and participants are thinking more about what they would say if they had a chance to play that part.

Basically so far in this workshop drama has been used in various forms to make a Bible story come alive: the Palm Sunday experience, the storm at sea, Jesus' parable about the workers in the vineyard and about the prodigal son, the role play of various Biblical episodes. Participation drama can be used for cognitive learning also and it is a very fun way to learn.

As an example, the following excerpt (See pg. 16) from the children's play A Jot And A Tittle, *What's A Jot And A Tittle?* by Judy Gattis Smith, published by Contemporary Drama Service.

SETTING: Your friend is standing, holding the poster and scratching his head. You come walking along carrying the felt-tipped pen.

FRIEND: There's something that's just not right here.
YOU: Hi, what ya doing?
FRIEND: I'm trying to read this poster but something's wrong.
YOU: Let me see. *(Study poster)* Oh, you need a jot.
FRIEND: A what?
YOU: A jot. *(Take felt tip pen and dot the "i")*

Lillle

FRIEND: Oh, you mean a DOT?
YOU: No, a JOT. A jot is the smallest possible element in writing in Aramaic.
FRIEND: *(Getting excited)* Hey, great! Wow! Oh boy! I've got a jot! *(Looks at poster)* But wait a minute — this still doesn't look right. *(Both of you study poster)*
YOU: You need a tittle.
FRIEND: A tittle? What's a tittle?
YOU: A tiny stroke or mark to help you tell one letter from the other. *(Takes felt-tipped pen and crosses the "t's")*
FRIEND: *(Getting excited)* Hey, I really have got a tittle. Oh boy! Hurray! Wow! Whooppee! I've got a JOT and a TITTLE! Now where have I heard that before?

Simulation Games have become an exciting new method of teaching for many age levels in the church.

Simulation games are re-enactments of some particular event in an attempt to bring this event into a present, lived moment. Theoretically we can learn and understand best about a situation by living through it.

An example of the above is the following excerpt (See pg. 17) from the play When We Were First Called Christians, *Thumbs Up — Thumbs Down*, by Judy Gattis Smith, published by Contemporary Drama Service.

THUMBS UP — THUMBS DOWN

INSTRUCTIONS: Have the class sit in a circle with a center arena left
bare. A volunteer or someone chosen by the leader comes to the center.
He is the "Christian". He is given a card with his instructions on it. He
has two minutes to convince the crowd of the argument on his card.
At the end of that time the verdict is up to the crowd. The leader turns
to the encircling class and asks: "Thumbs up or thumbs down?" The
class makes the response that they think is appropriate. The "Christian"
is either saved and joins the rest of the circle or is lead off to one side
and is out of the game. The "Christian" has the privilege of choosing
the next victim.

ASSIGNMENTS FOR "CHRISTIANS"

<u>NO. 1:</u> You are a 20th Century Christian and a member of the church.
The people in the arena think the Church has done many evil things
and has made many mistakes throughout history from the Inquisition
to our action in race relations today. You have two minutes to convince the crowd that they should not forsake the church for this reason
but remain loyal and supportive.

<u>NO. 2:</u> You are a 20th Century Christian and a member of the church.
The people in the arena think the church is made up of a bunch of
hypocrites. You have two minutes to convince the crowd that even
though there are hypocrites in the church we should not forsake it but
remain loyal and supportive.

<u>NO. 3:</u> You are a 20th Century Christian and a member of the church.
The people in the arena think the church is always asking for money
and they never see where the money goes. You have two minutes to
convince the crowd that they should not forsake the church for this
reason but remain loyal and supportive.

Along these same lines games can be used as a dramatic way of teaching. An example of this, the following excerpt from the play <u>Let's
Explore The Bible,</u> *Activity II: Jacob and Esau,* by Judy Gattis Smith,
published by Contemporary Drama Service.

ACTIVITY 2
(Observation games and the story of Jacob and Esau)

TEACHER:	Do you see when you look? Today we want to find out. We will also be hearing a new Bible story. Again we will use games to help us learn. Instead of "Simon Says" to give us instructions today we are using a drum *(or tambourine).* Whenever you hear a drumbeat, stop what you are doing and listen for instructions.
INSTRUCTIONS:	*(Teacher produces drum and illustrates)*

TEACHER: When I start beating the drum I want you to walk around the room and look very carefully at everything you see. When I give a single, loud drumbeat come sit down around me and close your eyes.

INSTRUCTIONS: *(Teacher beats rhythm on drum as children look around the room. Let them walk and look for about three minutes, then call them together with a drumbeat.)*

TEACHER: Now, are everyone's eyes closed? I am going to ask you some questions to see how well you saw things on your walk. Are there curtains in the room? What color are they? Do they have a pattern? How many doors are there? Are there any pictures on the wall? Of what? Where are the light switches? Are the windows open or closed? What kind of chairs are in the room?

INSTRUCTIONS: *(Add other questions that are appropriate to your room. Allow children to answer freely. For two final questions ask:)*

TEACHER: Who are you sitting by? How can you tell?

INSTRUCTIONS: *(Accept children's answers)*

TEACHER: We observed very well, didn't we? Let's make it a little harder this time. Everyone choose a partner. When I give a drumbeat everyone look at your partner very carefully. Notice all the things you can about him. What does he look like? And what is he wearing?

INSTRUCTIONS: *(Allow a few minutes for the children to do this. Then give a drumbeat.)*

TEACHER: Now partners must turn their backs to each other and each person must change three things about himself. *(For example: untie shoe, change hair part.)*

INSTRUCTIONS: *(Allow a few minutes for the children to do this)*

TEACHER: Now, face each other again and see if you find the three things your partner has changed.

INSTRUCTIONS: *(After the experience the partners may want to share with the entire group)*

TEACHER: Now, change partners and this time you must change <u>four</u> things about yourself.

1. First, on the drumbeat, study your partner carefully. . .
2. Now, turn your back and make your changes. . .
3. Now, try to discover what your partner has changed. . .

ACTIVITY 2 *(contd)*

INSTRUCTIONS:	*(This time it should be more exciting as the children tax their powers of ingenuity. Allow the children time to finish the game.)*
TEACHER:	On the drumbeat come and sit on the floor around me. How many of you were able to fool your partner?
INSTRUCTIONS:	*(Encourage children to share their experiences)*
TEACHER:	There is a story in the Bible of a young man named Jacob who changed some things about himself to fool his father.

LEADER: The ways to use drama in your teaching are endless. The teacher who is convinced that drama is important will find ideas coming from many sources. As we try it we will discover a whole new world of exciting teaching. Remember that drama in Christian Education is more concerned about the individual and what happens to him. Here we are not working on a production but are seeking to teach, to sensitize and to have a creative experience.

Give out worksheet (See pg. 21) for Thinking and Discussing. Group the teachers (pre-school, early elementary, elementary, youth, adult). Have a member of the Core Drama Group meet with each group. Work out the worksheet together and come up with specific plans for using drama in your Church School class at least once a quarter.

WORKSHEET

For Thinking and Discussing With Your Group

I. Select a Bible story for dramatization with your class. . .

SOME SUGGESTIONS of New Testament Stories for Dramatization are: *The Good Samaritan, Zacchaeus, Parable of the Talents* and *The Rich Young Ruler.*

(The ones in which the teaching is direct, rather than symbolic, are better than the ones in which the meaning has to be explained.)

SOME SUGGESTIONS of Old Testament Stories for Dramatization are: *Story of Joseph, David* and *Moses found by Pharaoh's daughter.*

(In choosing Old Testament stories to dramatize, make sure they have real significance for your class. Some are utterly unsuitable for present-day children either in subject matter or moral standards.)

ALSO, stories from your Church School materials may be selected.

II. LIST HERE your problems in attempting this dramatization:

TIME:

LEADERSHIP:

SPACE:

OTHER:

III. If you are convinced of the value of drama as a way of carrying teaching-learning into a student's life, you can overcome these obstacles. What are some steps you can take in overcoming your problems?

PAS-time Program

Our second direction for September is to begin an on-going dramatic program for children. What to do with the children during the 11 a.m. worship service is a concern of many congregations. One suggestion that seeks to answer this question, and at the same time meet the concern of your Drama Group for an on-going program, is to begin a program called PAS-time (Play A Story time). Children attend the 11 a.m. worship service with their parents and then before the sermon (in some churches this is during the singing of the second hymn) leave the sanctuary for special dramatic activities. They hear a Bible story and then in some dramatic form, play or act out the story.

Children ages 5 to 10 respond best to this activity.

Following are some topics for stories and suggested dramatic activities. You will want to use this as a framework from which to play your own program.

Children come for the fun of it, craving the personal expression and excitement associated with drama. They hear a Bible story and use a variety of dramatic forms. These dramatics are meant for the fun of putting on a show and having a learning experience. Since everyone usually wants a part, the plays must have expandable casts. If you run out of characters let children be trees or rocks, etc. . .

Keep the fun and excitement that accompanies drama. Truly Play A Story.

Children gather in the PAS-time room, seating themselves for the story of the day. Members of the Drama Group can serve as story tellers with parents on hand weekly to help with other activities. If possible have the children sit in a circle so that the leader can see every face.

The story teller will want to be very familiar with the Bible story, to cut long descriptive passages and to enjoy telling it. The Bible contains some of the best stories in the world and it is a joy to share these with our children.

Know the story well enough to read it with expression, only glancing now and then at the book. Even if you are telling the story, hold a Bible in your hands so the children will associate the story with the Bible. Portray emotions with your voice and facial expressions.

MONTH OF PARABLES WITH PANTOMIME

Suggested Stories: Good Samaritan — Luke 10:30-37
Sower and Seeds — Matthew 13:3-9
Parable of Talents — Matthew 25:14-30
Pharisee and Publican — Luke 18:9-14

Children listen to the story, trying to "feel" like characters in it. After the story they discuss the characters, recall the story line and act out the parable. The leader helps the children "feel" into the part with questions: "What kind of person was the Good Samaritan?" "The Priest?" "Who would like to be the Good Samaritan?" Choose someone quickly. If two children insist on the same character do the scene twice. Don't let the children argue. Get on with the acting. Encourage everyone to take part. Some can be rocks along the road or trees. Children love to get down on all fours and be the donkey. In the Pharisee and Publican children can be the crowd at the temple watching. Use your imagination and let the children offer suggestions.

Review the story again. Decide where the action will take place. "This is the field where the Sower sowed his seed" and pace it off. "This is where the robbers crouched." No attention is paid to dramatic technique, such as facing the audience. The entire emphasis is on acting like another person within the framework of the story.

Then the story is acted out. The leader must keep the story line moving and must stir up enthusiasm by example, either as a member of the audience or as a member of the acting group.

If there is time and if interest is still keen replay the story with different characters.

There may be time to do more than one parable each Sunday. Some additional parables that will work with this method are:

> Laborers in Vineyard — Matthew 20:1-16
> Two Debtors — Luke 7:41-47
> Wise and Foolish Builders — Matthew 7:24-27
> Guests at a Feast — Luke 14:7-11

MONTH OF POSE A PICTURE

Suggested Stories:
(Old Testament)   David and Jonathan — 1 Samuel 20
                   Esther — Book of Esther (condensed)
                   Deborah — Judges 4, 5
                   Ruth — Ruth 1-4 (condensed)

As children hear stories they are asked to create a picture in their minds. How do they see the story? Then using their classmates they pose-a-picture. Following is an example from the play Let's Explore The Bible, *Activity IV: David and Jonathan*, by Judy Gattis Smith, published by Contemporary Drama Service. Children gather in the story circle and hear the story of David and Jonathan. Following the story the teacher says:

ACTIVITY 4

TEACHER: You are going to show us the picture that was in your mind when we heard the part of the story about Jonathan warning David that he must leave. Instead of using paints or clays you are going to use people to create your picture — the children in our group.

You can choose whatever children you need to make your picture. Tell them exactly how you want them to stand or lie or kneel, what the expression on their face should be. The children in the picture must remember this is the artist's picture and do exactly what he tells you to do.

Children can be trees or rocks if you want them to.

No one in the picture can move or talk, so the picture has to tell us everything.

Help the rest of us see the story just like you saw it in your mind as you were listening to the story.

MONTH OF TAPE RECORDED PLAYS

Using a tape recorder can be another fun method of drama with children in your PAS-time program. Choose stories that have interesting sound effects and let the children come up with ways to create the sounds. If you have a large group of children divide into smaller groups with each group working out its tape recorder play. Then listen together to the play from each group.

Some stories that would work well with this method are:

Baby Moses in the bullrushes — Exodus 1:1 — 2:11
(Sounds of water, sounds of clanking jewelry, sounds of wind through bullrushes, etc.)

God speaks to Moses through the burning bush — Exodus 3, 4
(Crinkle paper to create sound of fire. Let a child speak through a megaphone as Voice of God, etc.)

Moses at the Red Sea — Exodus 14:1 — 15:21
(Sounds of chariots, armor clanging, water swirling, animals, running footsteps, etc.)

How God fed the hungry people in the Wilderness
(Bird sounds, cries of amazement, searching sounds, etc.)

MONTH OF PARABLES WITH PUPPETS

Suggested Stories: Prodigal Son — Luke 15:11-32
                          Lost Sheep — Luke 15:3-7
                          Unforgiving Governor — Matthew 18:23-35
                          Friend who came at Midnight — Luke 11:5-8

The children hear the story, create simple puppets, act out the story. (Details for a variety of puppets are found under the July chapter.)

For very simple ones use:

PAPER BAGS — Leave the bag (lunch bag size) unopened while making this puppet, since the folds are used to create an animated mouth. The bottom of the bag becomes the head. The top part of the mouth is drawn with the head; the bottom of the mouth is drawn below the fold. The hand goes into the bag and up and around the fold to make it open and close.

PAPER CUP PUPPETS — Make a hole in the cup for the puppet's nose. Be sure it is big enough for your finger to poke through. Draw eyes and mouth with felt marker. (Before you draw remember to rub the cup with a soapy cloth if it has a waxy surface.) Make three holes for your fingers in a tissue for the body.

Because PAS-time period is limited, quick, easy to make puppets are best. Material need only be construction paper, scissors, glue and crayons. There are:

WOODEN SPOON PUPPETS — The face is marked on the concave side of the oval with paint or magic markers in various colors. Hair of yarn or paper strips curled around a pencil may be added.

FINGER PUPPETS — Needed is a strip of paper about one inch wide and of the appropriate length to wrap around the fingertip and glue behind. A face of any character can be drawn on it.

Here are some things you can use to make puppets. Keep them all together in a box or on a table: construction paper, socks, old gloves, beads, pipe cleaners, felt markers, buttons, yarn, pencils, crayons, poster paints.

You may prefer to use a puppet play already written. For example, the following excerpt from the play Puppet Fun #1, *Samson The Strong Man*, by Marilyn Cram Donahue, published by Contemporary Drama Service.

SAMSON, THE STRONG MAN

ACT IV

SCENE: In the temple of the Philistines. Background of great stone pillars. At Center Front Stage are two pillars made of wooden building blocks, piled as high as possible. At Left Front Stage sits Samson, in chains. Philistines are milling around.

NARRATOR: Samson is really in trouble now, isn't he? He has been in prison a long time. The Philistines make him grind corn every day, so that they may have bread. There is one thing the Philistines haven't noticed. Samson's hair has been growing all this time. Now it is long again.

1ST PHILISTINE: Where's Samson, the strong man. Somebody go and get him, so we can make fun of him.

2ND PHILISTINE: Samson, the strong man? That's a laugh. Last time I saw him, he could barely walk.

3RD PHILISTINE: That's all the better. Go on and get him. We can put him next to the pillars and throw things at him.

2ND PHILISTINE: Good idea. *(Walks over and pokes Samson)* Get up and come with me. *(Looks at audience and laughs)* Heh, heh, heh . . . that is, if he's strong enough to stand up.
(Samson gets up and follows Philistines. His chains drag behind him. Philistines laugh and jeer, pointing their fingers at him.)

1ST PHILISTINE: Look at the strong man now!

2ND PHILISTINE: What's the matter, Samson? Didn't take your vitamins today?

3RD PHILISTINE: Ha! Ha! We'd better put him next to the pillar. We don't want him falling down, do we?

SAMSON: *(Puts hands against pillars and looks up)* Oh Lord, I know I've made mistakes. I've done some pretty foolish things, and I'm sorry. Please give me strength, I pray. *(Rumbling sound in background, increasing as Samson seems to gather his strength and stand up straight.)*

1ST PHILISTINE: Watch out! What does he think he's doing? *(They huddle together, frightened.)*

SAMSON: I'm knocking down your temple; that's what I'm doing. *(He pushes blocks, which topple over. Philistines fall to ground. Sound of crashing.)*

NARRATOR: And so Samson destroyed the enemies of his people. From that time on, he was remembered for his great strength, which God gave back to him when he needed it.

Another suggestion is the following puppet play in muppet manner, excerpt from Puppeteria II, *The Lost Lamb,* by Linda Thomas, published by Contemporary Drama Service. (See pg. 29)

Lily is a lamb, Freddy a frog, and Jose a donkey.

LILY: Oh, okay. *(Begins singing again)* "I'm a poor little lamb; Who has lost my way. Baa, baa, baa."

FREDDY: *(Dramatically)* Come back, little lost sheep. Come back with the rest of the sheep where you'll be safe.

JOSE: *(He pops Onstage)* Freddy, all those sheep are making me nervous. What if they decide to charge?

LILY: *(In exasperation)* Jose, we're trying to do a Bible story.

JOSE: THIS is in the BIBLE?!

LILY: Of course it is.

JOSE: Well, I guess it will be all right then. *(He pops Offstage)*

FREDDY: Okay, Lily, let's try again. *(Dramatically)* Come back, little lost sheep. Come back with the rest of the sheep where you'll be safe.

LILY: *(Also dramatically)* Oh, Good Shepherd, do you really care what happens to me?

FREDDY: Of course, I care.

JOSE: *(Pops Onstage)* Are you SURE this is in the Bible? It doesn't make any sense to leave all those sheep alone back there and come after just one.

LILY: It's a story Jesus told. He meant that God was like the shepherd.

MONTH OF ANIMAL STORIES FROM THE BIBLE

Suggested Stories: Noah's Ark: Genesis 5:1-9
Daniel in Lion's Den
Animals of Peaceful Kingdom: Isaiah 11:6-9
Animals mentioned in the Bible

Noah's Ark: Children hear the story from the Bible or use the tape "All Aboard the Ark" from Contemporary Drama Service. This tape gives children the opportunity to act out to music the movements of the animals boarding the Ark.

After hearing the story the children make simple costumes and act out the story.

Activity: Have scraps of material on hand for children to create suggestions of the animals; feathers, rope or twine for tails, cotton, pipe cleaners for whiskers, construction paper for scales or ears, paper cups for noses, paper egg carton for teeth.

Daniel in the Lion's Den: Again the children hear the story, make simple costumes and act out the story.

Costumes: Make lion costumes from oversized turtleneck sweaters with neck opening around the head and caught under the chin.

Animals of Peaceful Kingdom: Read the story. This is really an elaborated idea, not a story but pictures can be created in the child's mind.

Activity: Make box costumes of animals. Use grocery boxes large enough for the children to climb into. Draw animal features on the box. Add tail or snout or whiskers if you like. Add shoulder straps. Tie around a stick inside box so they don't pull through holes. Children get inside. Act out verses.

Animals Mentioned in the Bible: This week's format is different. There is no story. Children gather in a circle for instructions.

Animals: antelope, ape, ass, badger, bat, bear, bullock, calf, camel, cattle, chamois, cony, cow, deer, dog, dromedary, ferret, fox, goat, hare, hart, horse, jackal, lamb, leopard, lion, mole, mouse, ox, porcupine, ram, roebuck, sheep, swine, weasel, whale, wolf.

Assign one animal to each child. If possible have pictures of all the animals. In small groups (3 or 4) with adult helper look up the animal reference in the Bible or dictionary. Adults use Concordance to find passage. Talk to the children about the animal.

Activity: Using a carpet square 8" x 10" in size, create the face of your animal. Tape a tongue depressor on the back of the square to serve as a handle. Practice how your animal would move.

All the children come together in one large circle. They show their animal face, tell about their animal and show the class how it moves.

This can also be used as a guessing game. What animal am I?

Each player in turn acts out his animal and the others try to guess. You cannot say a word but you may nod your head "yes" or "no".

There are other resources available from Contemporary Drama Service that can help you in the PAS-time program.

ELEMENTARY CAN OF SQUIRMS, * a role playing activitity involving a child and an animal is a very good resource for this setting.

Let's Explore the Bible and Let's Be Dream Makers include activities using improvisational drama and fit well into this setting.

Drama — free, unstructured, fun, exciting, inclusive — is what we are trying to create.

* *Available from Contemporary Drama Service*

OCTOBER:

Family Night of Fun
Youth Play & Drama Games

It's October! Drama has now been introduced as an exciting new activity in your church. Teachers have made their first tentative steps into actual usage. Most likely your children have jumped in with enthusiasm to the PAS-time program. Now it's time to turn to the teenagers. Some have quite likely been a part of your entire planning process but now let's focus on them.

The importance of fellowship within the church and drama's role in developing it will be emphasized this month.

Many times opportunities to mingle with our fellow church members is limited to worship on Sunday morning. To deepen and round out our relationship with others we need informal occasions. We need to laugh together and eat together. We need to know each other in casual settings. We need to play together.

In our churches, youth are sometimes the invisible element. They are separated (often by their choice) from the rest of the church in many of our activities. During these years when youth are breaking away from their parents and seeking to find their own identity it is difficult to weave them into the whole fabric of the church. In some churches (let's face it) adults are more comfortable to keep youth at arm's length. The always accompanying noise, the general disorder, the animal energy, the inappropriateness of many of their responses, the unsettling questions pose a threat. This threat can become a dividing wedge in a church. Youth on one side and everyone else on the other side. It is easy for a youth leader to become popular if he/she decides to create an us-against-them attitude in a youth group. This can be very unfortunate for a church. How much better if this adolescent need for expression and individuality can be expressed and focused through drama. A bond between church and youth becomes cemented as youth present a drama for the church and are received with enthusiasm and love. Drama for youth also creates much outside interest and provides incentive for recreational gatherings.

Consider these possibilities: A church-wide family night of fun for all ages around Halloween with a pot-luck supper and a play put on by the teenagers. Create the mood by asking persons to come in costumes — all ages. Costumes are, after all, a form of drama in themselves and you may discover new talent for your drama group. Children especially like an excuse to wear their Halloween costumes on more than one occasion. If persons do not come in costume have on hand a supply of crepe paper in a variety of colors and let them create their own costumes there on the spot.

Before sharing the pot-luck supper you may want to have a parade of costumes for all to see.

Instead of costumes you may wish to use this opportunity to focus on drama games. You very likely have a new audience that has not tried drama before.

As the meal is finished, dishes are being cleared and the youth are getting ready for their performance a member of the Drama Group can lead in some table games that focus on drama.

Following are some suggestions. It is necessary, for these games, for persons to be seated at separate tables seating six to eight persons. Persons of all ages are seated at their tables. Each table works as a separate group.

Game I: Act out the following "I Am" passages in John's gospel: Bread of Life 6:35,48 — Light of the World 8:12,9:5 — Door of the Shepherd 10:7,9 — Good Shepherd 10:11, 14 — Resurrection and Life 11:25 — Way, Truth, Life 14:6 — Vine 15:1, 5.

1. Each table selects a runner.

2. Runners from all tables come to a central leader. Each runner is given a slip of paper with one of the "I Am" passages on it.

3. After reading their slip they run back to their table and act out the passage without using any words, only body movement and facial expression.

4.   The table that guesses first is the winner.

5.   Then all tables choose another runner and the game is repeated.

Game II: Pass It On

This game is also played at separate tables. Ask all persons to stand at the table forming a circle around the table.

The first person pretends to pick up something and pass it to the next person. It can be something heavy or light, big or small.

The second player tries to pass on the object the same way as the first in line did.

When the last player receives the object he guesses what he has. If he's wrong the other players help him. The first player tells if nobody guesses correctly.

Then the first player switches places with the last for a new game.

Items you will be passing are: (1) Something Moses would have handled, (2) Something David would have handled, (3) Something Peter would have handled, (4) Something Paul would have handled.

We are now ready for the play by the youth. A comedy is a good starting vehicle.

Plays of the slapstick variety could be given by teenagers in this dinner setting. If your Fellowship Hall has a stage this could be used or the center of your room surrounded by dinner tables.

The Parable of the Barren Fig Tree is a play that teenagers would have fun giving. In keeping with the Halloween theme it uses imaginative costumes. There is a Fig Tree with four creative suggestions on how a person plays a tree. There is a Bear which opens up interesting costuming ideas and three other characters. The short one act play is based on Luke 13:1-9. Blocking is very simple and there are few enough characters to allow you to work with two mikes. (Projection always seems to be a problem in local church drama. Most church fellowship halls have notorious acoustics and few local churches are willing to pay for extensive sound equipment.)

The background setting of a vineyard would give opportunity for youth who were not interested in acting a chance to be a part of the production. They could either draw a vineyard on large mural paper, build a set, or decorate themselves with vines and BE the vineyard.

An example of the dialogue excerpted from Five More Parables For The Present Imperfect, *The Parable of the Barren Fig Tree*, by Buck Kohr, published by Contemporary Drama Service follows:

THE PARABLE OF THE BARREN FIG TREE

SCENE: The action takes place in a vineyard. At the beginning, the Fig Tree is calmly sunning himself. The Gardener is pacing anxiously back and forth.)

FIG TREE: What are you so nervous about?

GARDENER: The boss'll be here any minute.

FIG TREE: So?

GARDENER: So what have you got to show?

FIG TREE: I have my good intentions.

GARDENER: What you're supposed to have is figs.

FIG TREE: Maybe I wasn't meant to bear figs.

GARDENER: What else could you be for? You're a fig tree.

FIG TREE: How do you know I'm a fig tree? Sometimes I think I might be an apple tree. Or an orange tree? Or a pretzel tree.

GARDENER: Pretzels don't grow on trees.

FIG TREE: They don't? I guess I must be suffering from an identity crisis. Tell the boss to send me to a tree psychiatrist.

GARDENER: A lumber mill's more like where you're going to get sent. What is it with you? I planted you in this nice vineyard. I've given you the finest soil, the finest fertilizer, the best sunlight! Why don't you bear fruit?

FIG TREE: Fruit! That's all you ever think about. I don't see why you can't appreciate my other qualities.

Another suitable play from Contemporary Drama Service is The Floundering Spaceship by Larry Glassco. This play also makes use of costumes which make it appropriate to the season. In addition it deals in a very creative way with the theme of Stewardship. In many churches the fall of the year is the time when financial campaigns are getting underway. This play is written in the style of the old TV series

Star Trek with the same basic characters. It is cleverly done and it deals with a theme of the relevance of the church — a theme with which youth always like to deal.

A floundering spaceship is found in space. The ship is the Church. The crew from the Starship Improvise explore this strange craft, examining the symbols and seeking an explanation of its Power failure.

The following are excerpts from The Floundering Spaceship.

THE FLOUNDERING SPACESHIP

OHOOPLA: So now we're inside the spaceship we just saw on the screen. . . It's certainly weird looking in here. . . I never saw a spaceship that looked like this. . . *(Pointing at window)* Look, there are the queer colored portholes we just saw from the outside.

SCOUTY: The crew doesn't seem to be on duty, Captain.

SPOOK: *(Aiming light meter at audience)* My tricorder reading shows very little signs of life here, Captain.

KOOK: Let's spread out and investigate. There might be some strange creatures in a spooky place like this. Careful everyone.

Finally they come upon the Minister who explains the Mission:

OHOOPLA: *(To Minister)* Sir, what is the mission of this ship?

MINISTER: Our mission is to carry a most important, high priority message from the GREAT PROVIDER OF THE UNIVERSE to all the people of the galaxy. Their whole existence and future depends on our success in accomplishing our mission. So we must get moving, or we fail Him who has given us the GREAT COMMISSION to go into all the galaxy to deliver the GOOD NEWS.

SPOOK: Since your ship is just barely moving ahead, it appears that you are not going to get your GOOD NEWS through to very many people!

MINISTER: It is the most important mission in all time and space. We need all the help we can get.

The crew goes to work on the malfunction. A clue to the problem is found in interrogating one of the church members.

SCOUTY: *(Enters with crew member)* Here is one of their crew members, Captain.

KOOK: Who are you, sir?

MEMBER: *(Sloppy, lazy & indifferent)* Name — A. Member; Rank — Pewman 2nd class; Position — *(Shrugs)* Typical crew member, I guess.

KOOK: Tell us, Mr. Member, what do you do to help make this spaceship go.

MEMBER: Well, my regular job isn't related to the propulsion of the ship. But I put in my weekday hours doing it — even though I'd rather be doing something else. Then on Sunday mornings I faithfully attend the Commander's briefing sessions — here on those hard seats. *(Points to pews)* I don't listen too hard but I figure my presence makes the rest of the crew think I'm doing my part.

KOOK: What else do you do?

MEMBER: Oh, I eat and sleep. I talk to the other crew members. And of course there are social activities and recreation. It all keeps me pretty busy.

SPOOK: Do you do anything else to help the spaceship accomplish its mission?

MEMBER: Well, if I have any time left over, after doing my own things, once in a while I try to help out around the ship where I can. It's mainly a matter of TIME.

KOOK: Do you have any special skills or TALENTS?

MEMBER: I bowl in the ship's league. *(Demonstrates with mime)*

KOOK: Talents useful to the running of the ship, Mr. Member.

MEMBER: Well, I guess I did have some useful talents when I was young. But to tell the truth it's been so long since I've used them, I'm not sure if I still have them anymore. You know how that goes, Captain. You get kind of rusty. . . *(Looks tired and bedraggled)*

Fortunately a solution is found and Power is restored.

A cast party given by the Drama group for the youth a few days later will further cement the growing bond of fellowship.

NOVEMBER:

Parades, Processionals, Pageantry, Choral Reading, Dramatic Scripture

November is upon us with a different feel in the church. The long season of Pentecost with its energy and verve is taking its toll. Outside the ground is hard, the year is old. There is ice in buckets. Trees are bare. Leaves, frost crisped, have broken from the boughs. Night owls' calls sound lonely. And yet nature in its starkness displays a certain loveliness. The beauty of the bone. Stripped of the paddings, the extras, it stands exposed. There is an awareness that perhaps God sees us this way. He looks arrow straight into our souls.

Surging within us is a need to give thanks.

It seems natural at this season that we move drama into the sanctuary.

Autumn is a time of mingled sadness and gladness. Leaves have fallen, greenery is faded brown, the year is dying. But it is also Harvest time, the season of ripeness and plenty. To capture this feeling — to capture this theme — is a challenge to your drama group.

Processionals and Harvest parades are a very old form of imaginative entertaining that have survived for ages. In ancient days, the Jews used to move from their homes to temporary camps in the fields while they reaped their crops and there they would celebrate the open air feast of the Ingathering. The ancient Romans held parades around their fields to celebrate the Harvest and long before this people walked in antiquity parades — processions, some of tremendous length. The participants engaged in these pilgrimages in the hope of moving a step closer to Heaven. Nothing written, spoken, sculptured or drawn can express pride, good wishes, or a sense of mass cohesion in quite the same way. A Thanksgiving parade or processional seems an appropriate way to gather up the feelings of this season.

It's easy to be a bored Christian at a Sunday liturgy. We can be physically present, emotionally absent and spiritually vacant with no trouble at all.

Our senses lie like old dogs by the fireside. We rarely think of rousing them as we follow the familiar rites.

Drama speaks to this condition. It offers an opportunity to revitalize. The color, the actions help us awaken, see things differently.

A parade is really anything that puts on a show and moves in a line. It can be the climax of a ceremony or the prelude to ritual. A procession is technically a less organized but usually a more solemn parade.

Many churches provide a perfect setting for a processional. The aisles lend themselves to dignified entrances, choir and organ create mood, the altar and perhaps stained glass windows make a background richer than any special scenery would. Pomp and pageantry — awe before God are what we are trying to create.

Perhaps you would wish to pick up some ancient traditions for your Harvest parade.

A letter written by Pliny the Younger to the Roman Emperor Trajan tells of solemn processions of early Christians who repeated, as they walked, "Christ our God to Thee we raise. . ."

A modern hymn known in most Protestant churches is "Fairest Lord Jesus". This would be an appropriate Processional hymn. As the people march in singing they could raise their arms on the ancient words "Christ our God to Thee we raise this our hymn of grateful praise". It could be used to begin the service of worship or conclude it or it could be enacted during the spot reserved for choir anthem.

Another ancient tradition tells of the singing of the Christian hymn "Jubilate" as early Christians walked, in solemn procession, through the corridors of the catacombs. This was supposedly accompanied by a marching pattern of three steps forward and one step back in solemn rhythm with the music. (Detailed instructions for this are included in "A Children's Thanksgiving Liturgy" in the book, Celebrating Special Days In The Church School Year, published by Contemporary Drama Service.)

Color could add to your processional. A lovely Thanksgiving banner designed by Michelle Zapel is available in pattern form from Contemporary Drama Service. There is an entire service which includes a worship service and banner presentation explaining the meaning of the symbols on the banner. This captures in a beautiful way the meaning of this season and the feelings we long to express.

Or you could create your own banner. Think in colors of amber, gold and brown. Let nature dictate the colors for this season. You may want to weave in a hazy blue like the ghosts of smoke. Red is the appropriate liturgical color.

Symbols you may wish to include are symbols of bountiful harvest, ripe fruit. The vine laden with grapes is a rich Biblical image. Wheat shafts, corn, apples, pumpkins, turnips can all be symbolized on your banner.

The overflowing cup from the image presented in the 23rd Psalm is appropriate at this season. The heaping baskets, the bulging barns, express the idea of a rich harvest.

The Eye of God symbol expressing God's power, majesty and omnipresence may be used or the Hand of God with thumb and first two fingers raised in the position of blessing. A hand, open and pouring forth blessings could be used.

All sensuous things to which a higher meaning is attributed, aside from the natural significance, are symbols. They become a sign serving to assist recall by suggestion if not by precise illustration.

Use your banner as a standard behind which the people march. This banner need not be limited to one celebration but carried in procession with other banners on festive liturgical occasions. A standard is important and is worth involving the time of a talented member of your drama group or congregation.

Instead of a banner you may wish to make a symbolic wheat sheaf to be used as a standard.

Following are instructions:

1. Take a double sheet of newspaper and tear it in half across the middle.

2. Roll one half up into a tube. When you get about 5" from end add other half sheets and roll it into the same tube.

3. Flatten the tube. Tear a cut down from the top about 4". Make four cuts or tears.

4. Then hold "trunk" of tube in left hand and reach right hand into center "leaves" and coax them gently upward so that the tube grows. It may be made bigger by adding another sheet.

5. Spray with gold paint.

In addition to a standard what will you carry? Baskets of fruit and vegetable produce — baskets of apples and leaves, shafts of wheat or grain, symbolic shafts of grain made from sculptured paper.

Besides people, color and a standard your parade needs music.

Ancient instruments will add excitement to your parade. If your procession moves out of doors the instruments should be easy to carry and make a noise loud enough for open air. You could parade around your church or march from one church to another.

Choirs could march along together and sing Thanksgiving hymns or anthems. Their choir robes, perhaps with colorful stoles, could mass and harmonize a portion of the parade.

Children's choirs could wear garlands of fall leaves and sing special anthems.

Parade marchers often toss things to bystanders. Outdoors children could toss leaves from baskets (real or paper ones).

A second idea to capture the feeling of Thanksgiving would be with a harvest liturgical dance. Perhaps your drama group could create such a dance. Women in free-flowing robes carrying baskets laden with produce could enter from as many aisles as your church has. If they are accompanied by a hymn, such as "For the Beauty of the Earth", a simple movement of raising the baskets in praise at the end of a phrase and then turning, walking gracefully and raising the baskets in the other direction at the end of the second phrase, could be worked out. Dignity, grace, solemnity are appropriate Thanksgiving responses.

It would be interesting to include small children in your dance or parade. It is an inspiring sight to see young children, even too small to master the steps, dancing alongside the adults, making a variety of mistakes but learning to praise the Lord with dance.

God, speaking to Moses and the children of Israel, after leading them out of captivity in Egypt, commands them to hold festivals three times a year. One of these is the Feast of the Ingathering. In the fall at the end of Harvest, God said, it is time to celebrate before the Lord.

We have focused this month on making a Thanksgiving banner or standard behind which persons march in thankful procession bearing symbols. We have discussed creating a Harvest dance as a way of celebrating before the Lord.

In addition, your drama group may wish to have a direct part in the context of the worship service.

Your drama group, moving with great sensitivity, can add much to your service of Worship.

We need to consider the variety of means and ways to get God's hopes and desires for us in the world across. We need to take time to re-examine all the parts of our worship service and see how much of it can be brought to life in another way without sacrificing its meaning.

We need to look honestly at the prospect that children find worship (particularly the Scriptures) dry and uninteresting; that cultural and linguistic differences make it hard for them to understand the timeliness of God's principles. We do not have to accept established pontifications about method, order and presentation of liturgy if we understand what the movement of worship is and are rigidly true to its purpose.

Drama speaks to the drabness and monotony that cloak many services of worship.

In many of our churches the participants feel they know what to expect at worship each Sunday. And, in some instances, the sameness palls, an apathy emerges no matter how strong the commitment or how deep the love. People who have joined a congregation with excitement and a desire to participate in reshaping God's world get disheartened after a while. Dull, drab and colorless could often describe our worship when our response more appropriately should be awe-struck and solemn, thrilled and enraptured.

Drama and dramatic actions bring freshness, color and the important joy of appealing to our visual, aural and kinesthetic senses. Jesus was never dull or drab. God's first gift to humanity was a rainbow.

Worship takes the point of departure from Holy Scripture. Your drama group can do much to make Scripture come alive. For example: a dramatic reading of Job 38-41, a dramatic reading of Jeremiah 20:7-18, a storytelling approach to the book of Daniel, (stories do not have to be literally true to express deep truth).

One of the functions of ritual is to express the significance of an event by heightened enactment. Symbolic actions can dramatize the word of the Lord. We raise the cup. We stand. We kneel. The book of Jeremiah is particularly rich in symbolic action: burying the linen waistcloth of Jeremiah (12:14 - 13:14), the wearing of a yoke (Jeremiah 27). The prophet Amos uses a plumb line to illustrate a truth to the people. In the same way our worship can become richer and more meaningful through the use of dramatic actions.

We formulate our faith in myriad ways. One way is to lift our voices together in praise and commitment in a speaking choir.

What is a speaking choir? It is a group of persons from eight to eighty (in age or in size) using their voices in combination to interpret Scripture or some aspect of the Christian faith.

A group doing a choral reading is like a choir except that they read rather than sing. The lines are divided among the readers. Some lines are read by everyone, some by individuals (called solo voices), some by part of the group.

A speaking choir could perform in place of a regular choir anthem or as a new way to read the Scripture during a worship service. Some churches turn the Gospel reading into a choral reading by having a Narrator read everything but direct quotations. The words of Jesus are said by a minister or priest and the words of others by other clergy or lay readers. The congregation acts as chorus, reading the words of the crowds. Without rehearsal most congregations respond magnificently to this type of presentation provided what they are expected to do is clearly explained to them.

The drama group, seated together in the congregation at center back or a front side section, can encourage proper tempo and depth of response to all the congregation's responses in the church service.

A choral reading including two voice choirs and solo voices would be in keeping with the dignity of your Thanksgiving service. A sample from Giving Thanks Is A Way Of Life, by Janet Litherland, published by Contemporary Drama Service follows:

GIVING THANKS IS A WAY OF LIFE

CHORUS B:	By sharpening our awareness, we could find many things for which to be thankful.
CHORUS A:	Like the singing of birds.
CHORUS B:	The baying of a hound.
VOICES 1, 2:	The patter of rain.
CHORUS B:	The clap of thunder.
VOICE 1:	A playing child.
VOICE 2:	Sunshine and shadows.
CHORUS B:	Changing leaves.
CHORUS A:	Pretty flowers.
VOICES 1, 2:	Bright eyes.
CHORUS:	And smiles.
CHORUS B:	The wind.
CHORUS A:	A baby's soft skin.
VOICE 2:	The cold snow.
CHORUS B:	A warm fire.
CHORUS A:	A kiss.
CHORUS:	Joy!
VOICE 1:	Solitude.
CHORUS A:	Peace.
CHORUS B:	Love.
CHORUS:	Life!
VOICE 1:	(Suddenly aware) Then this is what the thankful life is all about — being grateful for what is, not what isn't.
VOICE 2:	And, being aware of the goodness of creation and the encompassing presence of the Creator.
CHORUS A:	Not just being aware.
CHORUS B:	But reacting accordingly.
CHORUS:	That is, by giving thanks. It's a way of life. Let the redeemed of the Lord say so!

Choral reading works best in short phrases and sentences as illustrated on the preceding page. Variety in vocal tones and animated expression bring this type of drama to life.

A few other hints to make your group sound more professional:

1.   Begin exactly together on the first syllable.
     Have everyone exaggerate his breath intake slightly.
     Director should cue this with upswept arm and cue attack with downsweep.

2.   Exaggerate the vowels in a word for beauty, the consonants for a harsh sound.

3.   Watch the final "s". If they sound too hissed, cut them from the script of several members.

In addition to Contemporary Drama Service where do you find material? The Bible is an excellent source with many portions ideal for choral reading. For example, the Psalms, the last chapter of Job, arrangements from the Song of Solomon and Proverbs.

The hymnal of your denomination is a good source. Hymns with repeated phrases of "Alleluia" can be dramatically presented by reading the stanzas and singing the "Alleluias".

Your drama group may wish to create their own choral reading for Thanksgiving. Use the theme of God's unfathomed creativity, stressing God's imprint on every created thing, as a preparation for Praise.

Use the Fall imagery of barley, buckwheat, maples, apples, pumpkins, and leaves. Attempt in your writing and presentation to stir up praise and thanksgiving in all who hear.

Whichever method you use — procession, harvest dance, or choral reading — to bring drama into the sanctuary, strive to emphasize the grandeur of God's creation. Its awesome complexity and assuring simplicity — its power and order and fearful symmetry as impetus for a song of praise. Bring all your dramatic possibilities truly to lead your congregation in Thanksgiving.

DECEMBER:

Chancel Drama

Guide for Directors

It's December. Carols, old in our memories, set the mood. The early dusks somehow convey sweet suspense. Perhaps there is a first snow with a few very light flakes. In our churches the Advent season recalls how people waited for the coming of the Messiah. Prophets waited. Shepherds waited. The kings all waited for something yet to be. We find ourselves caught up in anticipation. Our private dreams and hopes intermingle with our historical yearnings.

Advent symbolizes all the times of expectation in our lives. Surging up are all the dreams and hopes for this life and the life to come that we experience throughout the year. Now, in this beautiful season these thoughts find expression. Christ is born in our lives each day as we open ourselves to his grace and love.

Advent is a time of looking both backward and forward. This is the season of sharing the hopes in which we were nurtured and the vision of that life in Christ. We look at our lives now and compare them with our dreams.

What better method than drama to capture these feelings. What better place than the sanctuary to express these thoughts.

This month we look at chancel drama — at using the people's setting for worship and ritual as a setting for church drama.

Let's take our cue from the season — let's dream!

When we enter the sanctuary we enter a spatial and temporal separation from ordinary life. It is a special place — a holy place — with special objects, special costumes, special words and sounds, special movements. All serve to heighten the impact of the worship experience.

All serve to make the enactment a symbolic one and a mystical one. Good chancel drama is aware of this. It brings about an order of things different to and higher than the one in which the participants live. It sheds radiance on the ordinary world. These heightening effects conjure up the life energies of the group, participants and spectators, active and passive.

Many show-type plays and even skits are labeled "chancel drama". These have no place in the sanctuary. The Fellowship Hall with a stage or theatre-in-the-round would be appropriate for these good plays.

But for the sanctuary — the place of worship — drama is almost an enactment of ritual. Drama used in the chancel is a different form of drama. It needs different production methods and different kinds of directing techniques. It should always be thought of as worship or at least, a preparation for worship.

A place of worship should not be constructed for theatre. The play which comes alive in a chancel should be played in the chancel as it is. This limits what can be done. The physical limitations of a sanctuary must always be given primary consideration in planning any kind of dramatic presentation.

Costumes are also different. They must heighten the experience, not stand alone. Each costume worn in the enactment of worship, whether it be choir robe or vestment is "put on" with meaning so that it becomes not a costume but a symbol in an active reality. This is good to keep in mind as you think of costumes for your chancel drama. Few plays have been written for sanctuary presentation. Biblical stories or characters that have values leading to deep searchings of soul and meditation may be dramatically presented.

The moral play of Everyman by Ann Dobie (a morality play adapted in length and language) is an example of chancel drama. Everyman is condemned by Death to give an accounting of his life. He seeks companions to go with him but all turn aside.

An excerpt from Everyman (now out of print, see Everyman II by Philip Bernardi), both published by Contemporary Drama Service follows on page 55.

STRENGTH:	Everyman, we will not leave you until you have finished this journey.
EVERYMAN:	Also, I am so faint that I can no longer stand. I must creep into this cave, there turn to earth and sleep.
BEAUTY:	What, into this grave? Alas! I cross all this out! Adieu! It is not for me to smother here.
EVERYMAN:	Now Beauty goes fast away from me. Beauty that promised to live and die with me.
STRENGTH:	Everyman, I too will forsake and deny you. This game I do not like at all.
EVERYMAN:	And you, too, Strength. He that trusts in his Strength, will be deceived at the end. Both Strength and Beauty forsake me, yet they promised me fair and lovingly.
DISCRETION:	Everyman, I will after Strength be gone also, for when Strength goes before, I follow after.
EVERYMAN:	When Death blows his blast, Beauty, Strength, and Discretion run full fast.
FIVE-WITS:	Everyman, we, too, must follow the others.
EVERYMAN:	Ah, Jesus, help. All have forsaken me!
GOOD-DEEDS:	No, Everyman. I will not forsake you. You will find me a good friend in your need.

To capture the feelings of the Season of Advent you might dramatically portray the great Biblical dreamers; Isaiah who dreamed of Peace, Moses who dreamed of a land of milk and honey, John the Baptist who dreamed of a world where people did not hurt each other, and Mary who dreamed of Emmanuel.

If the sanctuary is regarded as a platform for a sermon then a play can be produced on this platform. Backdrops, curtains and footlights are not necessary for good dramatic performances and have no place in chancel drama.

Be aware that when these theatre aids are taken away the actors become much more prominent. The quality of the acting is primarily important. This is the place for your most accomplished actors from your drama group.

An example of a play from Contemporary Drama Service which puts emphasis on this kind of acting ability follows (page 56). Excerpt is from Tyndale by John Stuart Anderson.

TYNDALE: *(On the departing ship)* This is the moment I have
always feared. Have I the strength to hold the
course that lies before me now? I was born alone
and grew alone between the changing moments of
the years. In solitude I took to scholarship; alone,
became a priest, my way to God as lonely as a
miser's tomb. And God is final solitude. The circle
moves and I the center cannot escape the barrier
between me and the next, so now I go to work in
solitude. Friends I've had, beloved friends, yet none
could break my solitude. But from that solitude has
grown the single purpose of my life. One step would
take me back to land where I might live as other men,
without this vision of a book. I'd go into the country-
side, and live beneath the forest oak, or by the willow
in broad fields and pray in antiphon with streams
and every pleasant country sound across this fair,
beloved land to which I never shall return. Farewell
to life, to love farewell.

The skill of the director of this type of drama is all important. If the
play is to come alive in a worship setting the director must have a
sense of worship. He/she must have a "feel" for the place that will
give the direction a tone, a quality that is unique. He/she must be a
better director because of the conditions of the place.

Remember the functions of chancel drama differ from those aspects
of theatre which serve to entertain. The functions are more mystical.

1.   The chancel drama expresses the significance of an event by a
     heightened enactment.

2.   It uses the setting — pulpit, organ aisles to set a serious tone.

3.   It sheds light on spiritual mysteries. A new technique may evolve
     when the conditions and purposes of the production are thor-
     oughly understood. There will be new uses of the voice because
     of projection requirements.

There will certainly be music, with larger usage and different usage than in traditional drama.

There may be an integration of liturgical dance, music and drama to produce this unique form which will be called chancel drama.

It will undoubtedly appeal to the senses — visual, aural and kinetic.

These chancel dramas are yet to be written. Perhaps you, reading this book are the one to do the writing.

Conditioned by this season, we have dreamed and envisioned a new form of drama, better defined perhaps as a dramatic enactment of worship. Since traditionally this season encompasses dreams and reality let us be very practical now and look at the nitty gritty. What could be a practical, general guide for this special chancel drama director?

A. **Where do we begin?**

1. Considerations in selecting a script.

   a. Purpose of play. Why? What do you want to say?
   b. Probable audience. Who?
   c. People to do the play. Who? How many? Experience? Availability?
   d. Place of performance. Technical and practical possibilities of your chancel.
   e. Dates of performance. How much time available to work?

B. **You have chosen your script. Now what?**

2. Script study.

   a. General reading. Keep notebook of all ideas.
   b. Work readings. With or without specific actors in mind. With audience in mind. With accurate knowledge of physical possibilities.
   c. Work out general or complete blocking.
   d. Prepare rehearsal and production schedule.

C. **Get going.**

1. Tryouts

    a. Announce by all available means the time and place.
    b. Offer private readings to those who are very interested but fear the public tryout.
    c. In some cases you may wish to choose the cast without tryouts.
    d. If tryouts are your route, be organized.
    e. Make people feel comfortable.
    f. Look for voice differences, physical differences, imagination, willingness and ability to take and carry out directions.
    g. Always allow a person to read for a specific role if requested.
    h. Explain thoroughly the rehearsal schedule and how the actors will be notified.
    i. Explain as much as you feel is necessary concerning your interpretation of the play.

D. **The Work**

1. Schedule

    a. Work out in as much detail as possible the exact date and time for rehearsals in order not to waste actors' time.
    b. Insist on punctuality.
    c. Indicate when lines are to be known.
    d. Call any actor who misses a rehearsal.
    e. Take into consideration the individual personalities of each actor.
    f. Try to make the rehearsal a meaningful experience in itself.
    g. Have dress rehearsal as close as possible to the public performance.
    h. Have invited "audience" at dress rehearsal.

E. **This is it!**

1. Performance

    a. Begin on time.
    b. Have all actors in the church by at least one half hour before scheduled performance time.

JANUARY:

Play Reading, Write your Church's Historical Drama

January is a snug month. It's a month of curling up and keeping warm. Short days, grey skies, crackling fires and purring radiators add to the intimacy of this month.

January is a good month for your drama group to investigate play reading.

Your group has been active in all aspects of the church: leading the children in dramatic activities, encouraging the youth with role play and youth drama, bringing dramatic moments into the sanctuary.

Now come back together as a small group and use this month to meet for the purpose of reading plays. Forget the equipment for a formal drama group — just read good plays together with different people often reading the same part — studying the characters and the characterizations and discussing the play as well as the issues and problems with which it deals. This can be a tremendously stimulating activity for your group. This technique makes it possible for a group to become familiar with a number of good plays without the time and effort of a formal production.

For this form of drama to be most effective persons with at least some experience in drama or a feel for dramatic reading should take part. A poor reader could defeat the purpose.

In play reading the readers keep themselves close to the rest of the group. For variety you could use identification signs with character's names but even this is almost too much structure. The important thing is the reading. This must be done with understanding, proper inflections and expressions, with readers picking up their cues on time and projecting voices properly. It is a fascinating experience to have different persons read the same part and see the different aspects of the character emerge. For even though a character may be strictly defined by the author, the actor always projects something of himself into the script, breathing life into the printed pages.

An interesting experience for your group would be to read the play, The Sobbing Stone by Dick Charlton. After reading it together with various persons taking the parts, listen to the tape of the play also available from Contemporary Drama Service. Where did the professional actors on the tape read lines differently from your group reading? What new meaning emerged?

A home setting seems to work better for play reading than a church school room as we emphasize intimacy and closeness and sharing of our ideas and ourselves.

After an evening or two you may want to add variety to your play reading. The variations to this form of drama are almost infinite. You may feel a need to get up and move your character, pantomiming actions and suggesting imagery props.

The play, The Tenants and the Landlord is more effective with the movements suggested in the script. The characters begin seated in an inverted "V" shape. Following is an excerpt from The Tenants and the Landlord, by Martin Doering, published by Contemporary Drama Service.

THE TENANTS AND THE LANDLORD

(Voice F Enters, friendly, easy-going; carrying a large basket.)

VOICE F: Hello! The master sends his greetings, and he sends me to collect some of his rent. He doesn't need all of it; just a portion will do.

VOICE C: Welcome, sir. *(Speaks sarcastically)* Your presence here is greatly appreciated. But I'm afraid that we are not able to comply with your request.

VOICE B: Our harvests have been poor. We barely have enough to keep our families alive.

VOICE D: But here is part of the rent. *(Hands "F" an invisible "something" but lets it fall before "F" takes it. "F" has to pick it up.)* Sorry to be of so much trouble.

VOICE A: And here is my part. *(He deliberately drops "something" on the ground and laughs as "F" stoops to pick it up.)*

VOICE C:	I have found part of my rent. *(She throws "something" at "F" who winces as it hits him. The tenants laugh out loud.)*
VOICE D:	Here is some more. *(Savagely, "B" throws "something" at "F", who is knocked to his knees. The tenants are mocking and laughing, becoming violent in their scorn.)*
VOICE D:	Here, have part of my wall! *("D" has a large and heavy "something" that he throws at "F", who falls to the floor. The tenants turn to face the back of the audience and yell.)*
VOICES A, B, C, D:	Curse you, landlord! *(After mutual congratulations, they return to their places, and face away from audience. "F" rises slowly, retrieves the basket, and painfully stumbles out.)*

Another variation to your play reading might be to have very simple material on hand to suggest costumes — scarves or hats or robes may help an actor express his character.

Most often play reading is followed by discussion but needless to say, not all plays will elicit discussion. If you are planning discussions following your reading, look for a play that cuts deep or presents conflicting points of view.

Your group could spend the entire month studying one play. For example T.S. Elliott's play, Murder in the Cathedral. Members of the group could each have a copy of the play to study at home. Some might want to do correlated reading on the life of Becket and the social situation of the day. Discussion would center around the relationship of church and state (then and now) and a definition of the role of the church in society.

At the other end of the spectrum your drama group might like to get together to read comedies and silly skits just for the fun of laughing together and expressing yourself creatively. Many of the plays by Peg Kehret from Contemporary Drama Service fall into this category.

You may find that the response elicited from your play reading is neither discussion nor fun but sets a mood for worship or directed meditation.

Those who love drama will enjoy exploring a wide variety of plays through play reading.

Let's move now in an entirely different direction for January. In this month when a bitter, chilly day can suddenly turn soft and still with a covering of snow, a long range drama idea for your church (uniquely yours) can begin to emerge. You may wish to begin an historical drama of your particular church. This is a huge project which includes envisioning the idea, researching the background, writing the drama, casting the play and producing it. The fostering group for this project may be your drama group or another select committee concerned with your particular history and archives.

Perhaps there is an anniversary coming up for your particular church or for one of its founders or a founding family and you are thrashing about for some special way to celebrate this occasion. What vehicle better meets these needs than drama? Perhaps your purpose would be to stimulate a sense of self-esteem and pride in your particular church. Perhaps you long to re-awaken and energize spirit and morale in your group.

If you choose drama then you must be dramatic. Guard against the tendency to spout facts and records however great they may be and interesting to you. Historical drama begins with a fabric either of facts or of legendary happenings but the dramatization must use material which can stir an emotional response. Facts are your basic material but out of theatrical necessity there will probably be varying degrees of license with the facts. As a writer you will have to select, arrange, and modify the data of personalities and events.

There are two major themes around which you can develop an historical drama for your church.

One is a drama which focuses on the life of an actual person, your founding minister, for example. This person should have an uncommon intensity of purpose and should run into conflict and obstacles in carrying out this purpose. Barriers must be equal to or stronger than the leading character's exertions or the drama will lack sufficient struggle. The character must fall and rise again, must fail but continue in order to arouse sufficient drama to be entertaining. The central character must be real enough for us to identify with, yet have about him a touch of magnificence whether in the final act, he succeeds or fails.

Another focal point for your historical drama might be an event (natural or man-made) — a fire, a flood, a war, the decision to move the church from one area to another — some moment of crises or event which shows courageous performance in the face of pressure. People, doing the best they can under terrible pressure, exhibiting great heroism, idealism and endurance. The drama could then be created out of the effect this event had upon the persons confronted by it.

Having chosen your character or event decide on the form your historical drama will take.

It could be a pageant drama with a series of loosely linked episodes evolving around the main character or event — a panoramic view so to speak. Or it could be a one-act biography performed on a stage.

You might fashion your historic drama after some of the large outdoor dramas presented throughout our country.

It would be a thrilling experience for your church to recreate history rather than record it. A dramatic re-enactment of your particular heritage would be an exciting and unique contribution of a drama group.

And though this project would take several months or years January might see its beginning — an idea suggested, an event recalled, a method proposed, a project begun.

FEBRUARY:

An All Church Revue
Feet Drama, Skits, Stunts, etc.

By February some of us are becoming stir crazy. The cold and dreary weather has gotten to us. This is the time for wild and crazy drama to release our pent up energies, our contained imagination. Back we go into the church setting. We interact with our wild and crazy youth, our leaping and jumping children.

We look for new ways to do things, the sillier the better. This is the time for "Feet Theatre" and "Finger Drama". Outrageous costumes, puns and corny lines, wildly imaginative tales are in order.

Our liturgical year and historical tradition are in tune with these feelings. Just before Lent we celebrate the Mardi Gras. Before we turn inward for six weeks of contemplation we are on exhibit — extroverted, obnoxiously loud and silly.

Plan an all-church revue for this month. Let each group in the congregation (adult, Sunday School classes, youth groups, women's circles, etc.) take part in a vaudeville type production. Call it "Talent and Stunts" if you like. Perform and intersperse acts with lots of music. Players can really let their hair down with solo performances, original skits, dance routines. If your church has a Fellowship Hall with a stage this is the place for your Revue. Use homemade signs on easel to introduce each act and be sure you have a good Master-of-Ceremonies.

Your group might like to create one large colorful backdrop for an entire show. Use backdrops with strong color — drabness has little appeal. Intense colors mean more than shades or hues and unreal or impractical colors have the greatest appeal. Use the warm side of the color wheel. An abstract design will work best.

If your groups have trouble coming up with ideas here are some to prime the pump:

Let one group (your youth?) produce "Feet Drama". Choose a story or parable from the Bible. The actors are persons' feet decorated with felt tip pens to make faces or animals (eyes on soles of your feet, mouth on heel and nose somewhere between).

Cut the back out of a large cardboard box. Cut holes in the other side for feet to stick through. Staple a piece of cloth over the inside of the opening. This forms your stage and curtain. "Actors" sit on the floor and stick their feet through the curtain. The feet bob up-and-down and side-to-side to accompany dialogue. It is best to have only two foot actors on stage at one time.

Give another part of your body equal time with "Finger Drama".

Using the same stage, stick your hands enclosed in gloves, through the opening. An example of the type of drama you can do follows. (Remember, in this vaudeville style production serious thoughts and comedies mix. Serious talent and silly acting stand side by side on the bill for the evening.)

MEDITATION WITH GLOVES:
The Prayer of St. Francis

(Two hands in gloves appear Onstage)

READER: Lord, make me an instrument of thy peace. Where there is hatred — *(Hands clutched in fists)*
Let me show love, *(Hands open, palms up, receiving.)*
Where there is injury — *(Right hand falls limply)*
Pardon. *(Left hand pats right hand in comfort)*
Where there is doubt — *(Hands rotate back and forth from wrist)*
Faith. *(Hands clasp each other in handshake)*
Where there is despair — *(Right hand in fist)*
Hope. *(Left hand goes to fist and uncurls the fingers very slowly)*
Where there is darkness — *(Hands walk in opposite directions)*
(Continued)

READER: *(contd)* Light. *(Hands move slowly together until they touch palm to palm)*
Where there is sadness — *(Hands hang limply forward)*
Joy. *(Both hands up, wiggle all fingers very fast.)*

You might even want to try "Eyebrow Drama". Eyebrows have three movements: Up, Down, and Middle. Choose an old fashioned waltz in 3/4 time and as the music plays, the class performs with the eyebrows: Down, Up, Up. Down, Up, Up.

Use a director if you like to keep all eyebrows working at the same time.

Spectacular, fanciful, colorful costumes are appropriate for your Revue. The play, We're All in this Together by James Inman uses characters dressed as fruit. Casting suggestions include costuming one as an aging grape, another as a banana, another a strawberry, etc. Costumes can be made from papier-mache, foam rubber with a cloth covering or whatever your imagination devises. An example of dialogue from the play follows:

WE'RE ALL IN THIS TOGETHER

ALBERT: *(To Carolyn)* Plenty of time! What do you mean, plenty of time? Lady, we're all on the verge of being devoured and you say she has time! Do you realize what's at stake here?

CAROLYN: Of course I do, but it's all part of living and you'll have to accept it.

SUSAN: *(To Albert)* It couldn't be as bad as you make it anyway. My parents and theirs before them have gone through it.

ALBERT: *(To Susan)* Have you ever seen anyone carameled or maybe bobbed at?

SUSAN: No, I haven't.

ALBERT: Well, I have and it's not a pretty sight! Don't think for a minute she washed you off for "your" health.

BILL: I admire your flavor son, but aren't you being a bit tart?

ALBERT: Yes, and all for good reason. I don't find the prospect of being made into preserves very appetizing.

GLADYS: What makes you so hard anyway?

ALBERT: Because all of you are blind to things happening around you.

BILL: Easy now, son, let's not start rocking the bowl.
CARL: He's getting under my skin.
ALBERT: You're all alike. Your only goal in life is to get ripe and join that big fruit salad in the sky — well, not me. There's more to life.

Another idea is to have one class simply do a parade of outlandish costumes. Does your church have a Lost/Found box? Most churches do and, by the end of a year (or several years) there is an interesting accumulation of hats, gloves, pocketbooks, jackets, etc. This is an excellent beginning point for your costume parade. For elegance add discarded evening dresses and dressing gowns. These can be bought cheaply at rummage sales. Old sheets, pillowcases, worn men's shirts, threadbare blankets and worn bedspreads form yardage for any number of costumes. Use these to create an impromptu parade of people through the ages — cave men, Romans in togas, etc. Old pajamas and long underwear offer many possibilities. Hats and wigs are always winners.

A mock fashion show like the popular <u>Paris (S.D.) Festival of Fashion</u> by LeRoy and Marjorie Koopman might be just the thing for your group. It is available from Contemporary Drama Service. Here is a sample of the narrator's fashion spiel.

PARIS (S.D.) FESTIVAL OF FASHION

(Model 2 wearing box coat — large cardboard carton — Enters)

NARRATOR: Very popular in Paris this spring is the box coat. Its simple, straight lines emphasize the importance of attractive packaging. Instead of the traditional buttons and zippers, this number comes with glue and stapler. The buyer has a choice of colors — light brown, dark brown, beige and brownish-white. The price is a fabulously low $98.99, plus freight charges. Thank you, _____.

> *(Model 3 wearing tissue gingham — toilet tissue*
> *streamers — Enters)*

NARRATOR: Our next dress is the tissue gingham, modeled by
(contd) _____. This number has really
made a clean sweep of Paris this spring. Many styles
are available, at various prices. The Charmin is $8.98;
the Northern is $9.98; and the Doeskin super-soft is
$12.98. Unfortunately, this dress cannot be dry-
cleaned or washed. Thank you, _____.

Another idea is to have a Narrator read a crazy skit and the audience
joins in by making appropriate responses. An example follows:

THE WILD WEST WEAKLING

The narrator reads and the group responds. Divide into six smaller
groups and assign one of the noises to each group. Before reading,
have all groups practice their noises, including the final kiss.

Horses *neigh*; Shots go *pow! pow!*; Hoppy noise is *"hurrah"*; Dirty
Villains *hiss*; Minnie says *"Ah-h-h-h"*; Friendly Indians say *"How"*
and *shake hands with each other.*

NARRATOR: Here my friends, is a story of the Old West. In the days
when men were men, women were women, *Horses* were *Horses* and
the folks aimed to keep it thataway.

In this same country grew up a small boy, The Wild West Weakling.
He sent off for a muscle building course and became the strongest
man in the country. His name was *Hoppy Long.* (They called him this
because of his strange hop, caused by dropping a muscle builder on
his foot.) He had a *Horse* named Ivory, and they were close as
brothers. (You could always tell them apart because the one with the
long tail was Ivory.)

Among their closest friends were the *Friendly Indians.*
(Continued)

NARRATOR: *(contd)* In the same country also were some *Dirty Villians* and were they stinkers. They never bathed and furthermore they stole *Horses.*

Our hero's girl was the lovely *Minnie Ha Ha,* daughter of old Chief Pow-Pow. The *Dirty Villains* were afraid of our hero but one day when he went to the city to get a store-bought suit, they decided to steal in at night, steal the *Horses;* and steal away. *Minnie* overheard them making plans, so she sprang on her trusty *Horse* and started to warn her lover. In a moment the *Dirty Villains* captured her and rushed her to their hideaway.

Two *Friendly Indians* saw it all, and they rode to warn *Hoppy.* Would he get back in time? When he heard, he said, "Why those dirty *Villains,* I'll lick 'em single handed." As he rode on he said "No I'll use both hands." When he neared the robber camp, he yelled to *Minnie Ha Ha,* "I'll save you". The robbers took a *Shot* at him. He *Shot* back. Then he *Shot* again. Things got lively. They *Shot* and *Shot* and *Shot.* He *Shot Shot Shot Shot.* They *Shot* and *Shot* and *Shot Shot Shot* right back. Soon they ran out of *Shots* and one of them called out "Boys we're all washed up." *Hoppy* and the *Horse* Ivory did the trick.

That's about all. *Minnie Ha Ha* helped *Hoppy* take the *Dirty Villains* to jail, where they got their just desserts. Soon afterward *Hoppy* rewarded the *Friendly Indians* and then he gave his trusty *Horse,* Ivory, some sugar. And of course, no good western ends without having the hero give the heroine a nice big juicy *Kiss* (each person kisses back of hand). *

Don't forget the possibility of stunts. Original ones are best but some of the old favorites from fifty years ago will be brand new to this generation which finds its entertainment in TV and computers.

Persons walking across stage holding signs saying: "Time Passes", "Waiting for the Train" are classics that can be updated. Television commercials open up a whole range of possibilities for stunts.

Acting out a song with very literal, exaggerated motions and oversized props becomes a stunt. Descriptive words like "lost my heart", "eat your words", "dropped her eyes" — all of these suggest their own actions. Remember the cornier the better. This is "silly" time.

---

* "Wild West Weakling" from <u>Skit Hits</u> by Helen and Larry Eisenberg, copyright 1952. Used with authors' permission.

An interesting stunt could be to have a class create a forest scene from scratch using the persons in the class as scenery and animals; trees, squirrels, etc. It could begin with: "One day I was walking along and suddenly I found myself entering a forest. First I saw — etc." This idea could be used to create many different types of scenes.

Of course Westerns and Detective Stories always make good take-offs, as do Space Scenes.

Scenes from the life in your church might be interesting: The Choir meets, a Church School class of rowdies, a meeting of the Official Board, a Nursery Class (played by your 60+ group).

You might want to include a storyteller in your Revue. There is an ancient saying, passed down from one generation to another, stretching far back to a time when men worked hard hunting, trapping and fishing, where people lived with few books or none. There is a saying from those days, "To keep men from being weary-hearted, a kind god created the storyteller."

The stories should be of the folk tale variety or stories which are really long jokes with a good punch line. They can be stories where the audience joins in the action or a story with a repeated refrain that is used so much the audience starts joining in. Aesop's Fables and folk tales with a morale could be used and acted out. For example:

> A farmer who lay dying called his sons and said, "My sons
> I am about to die. You will find hidden in the vineyard all
> I have to give you." Thinking their father had buried a treas-
> ure the sons forgot their grief and dug and dug every inch
> of the vineyard. No treasure came to light but so well was
> the soil tilled that the vines yielded a rich crop which was
> exactly what the wise old farmer wanted.

The possibilities of an all-church revue are as varied as the members of your church. You could use: cheerleaders, flag twirlers, solos on piano and other musical instruments, dramatic monologues, folk dances from other countries in costume, or group singing that follows the bouncing ball.

Resources from Contemporary Drama Service to further help you with ideas include: An Old-Fashioned Soap Opera by Paul Leslie, Wait 'Til The Sun Shines, Nellie by Craig Sodaro or any of several other melo-dramas.

MARCH:

Intergenerational Drama Study on the Theme of Lent & Easter

March is a month of anticipation. It is a teasing month with glorious Spring days taunting us in a week of Wintery days. It's like prelude music that builds us up to something glorious that is about to happen. We see buds on trees not opening yet — but almost. We see hints of green barely discernible under brown leaves and ground cover. A peek, a promise — but not yet. There are still snowy days to plod through — dreary days to confront — a daily life journey to continue. March reminds us in its dramatic, fickle way of the uncertainties of our lives and we realize anew that we, in ourselves, are powerless but the Promise is there.

How appropriate that the season of Lent comes at this time. Lent, in our churches, is an inward-looking season. We reflect on the mighty acts of God in history and His acts in our lives. We study the temptations of Jesus and struggle through our own forty days to Easter. We look to the vehicle of drama as a teaching/learning device this month to help us know by involvement the meaning of these days.

The drama suggestion for March is for an intergenerational drama study for the six weeks of Lent.

Intergenerational sessions, involving all age levels, are meaningful ways of learning in the church school. Intergenerational study affirms that the community of faith learns from all ages. We study together about our faith. We explore it together. Each age shares its unique insights.

Intergenerational study can occur on Sunday morning during church school, at family night sessions, on retreats or whenever the community of faith gets together to learn.

Each of these Lenten sessions uses drama to lift up a theme of Lent and involve students in a lived moment. Discussion questions or creative activities are also rightly a part of the sessions.

Many adults know what Easter means to them but can they express these beliefs in words that have meaning for children?

Teaching about Easter to children is not easy. Children identify much more readily with Christmas — a baby in a manger — gifts — music. They can understand Jesus as a person who loved people and helped them. But what about the Jesus who was hated so much that some people wanted to kill him? We often gloss over this. It is easier to teach about Resurrection than it is about the Crucifixion — even here when it comes to teaching children we are not exactly sure what to say.

"Christ Is Risen" is the central affirmation of our faith. To study and teach Jesus' life and ministry without emphasis on his crucifixion and resurrection is to treat Jesus as just another man who did good things in his lifetime and nothing more. Such limitations water down our faith.

Therefore, in the great tradition of our heritage as Christians, we all must come to grips with Jesus, the Christ, the Resurrected Lord.

Session 1 Theme: The Whole Life Of Jesus

Leader welcomes persons of all ages:

Today we are beginning a journey together — a journey through a period of time called Lent to a destination called Easter.

Easter is the greatest celebration in our church. We need these six weeks of Lent to help us get ready for this celebration. We need Lent so that we can remember what Jesus went through and what others have gone through in His name.

Easter, as you know, celebrates the death and resurrection of Jesus Christ. But we can't really understand it until we look at the whole life of Jesus — his birth, his life, his teachings, his relationships, his death and resurrection. All of these belong together.

Today we begin at the source. We turn to the Gospel accounts of the life and teachings of Jesus.

(Present narrative: <u>We Know About You Jesus</u>. Parts may be assigned before time or read spontaneously. Slides of children's artwork accompany the presentation. Someone will need to set up and show slides.)

Here is a sample of the narration of this Contemporary Drama Service presentation:

WE KNOW ABOUT YOU, JESUS

NARRATOR 1: *(Still acting Herod)* We will kill small babies only. But! We must take no chances. Slay all babies up to two years old. Do you captains understand the order?

NARRATORS 2 & 3: *(Together)* We do, your excellency. *(SLIDE #7 OFF)*

NARRATOR 1: *(To Audience as an aside)* Now I'm just me again. *(Narrating again)* That was how King Herod decided to kill the Baby Jesus. But even though his soldiers did kill many, many children in Bethlehem, he did not kill you, Jesus, because... *(SLIDE #8 "An Angel Talks To Joseph In A Dream")*

NARRATOR 2: ...because an angel came and warned your father, Joseph, while he was sleeping. He said: "Take the Baby Jesus and go to Egypt where Herod cannot find you" . . . And Jesus, *(Looking up again)* are you still listening, Jesus? . . . well, Jesus, your father, Joseph, did take you and Mary to Egypt where you were safe. . . *(SLIDE #8 OFF)*

Activities for the First Session:

Following the narrative the group joins together in the following responsive reading:

(Divide the group into two parts, Group I and Group II.)

PLEASE TELL US WHY

TOGETHER: Please tell us why, God. . .

GROUP I: Why Jesus was kind to people that others did not like.

GROUP II: Why He healed His enemies as well as His friends.

GROUP I: Why He didn't ask for something in return for His acts of love.

GROUP II: Why He didn't feel He had to be like other people to be accepted.

GROUP I: Why he didn't hate people who tried to make Him look foolish. . .who tried to punish Him.

TOGETHER: How can we be like Him?

TOGETHER: Please tell us why, God. . .

GROUP I: Why everyone in the world has not chosen to follow the ways of Jesus.

GROUP II: Why only a very few people in our school, our church, our home really follow the lessons of Jesus.

GROUP I: Please tell us, God, how we can learn to think and act in His Spirit of giving love.

GROUP II: Please tell us how just one of us can make the start that will help others follow. . .

TOGETHER: the ways of Jesus, our Savior.

Divide intergenerationally into groups of six or eight persons. Write a prayer expressing gratitude to God for Jesus. As a group share ideas, each person (all ages) gives a thought to add to the group prayer.

Close with the group reading together:

WE THANK YOU GOD FOR JESUS

PARENTS: Let us remember Jesus and give thanks for him.
CHILDREN: Jesus was friendly. He talked with people and tried to make them happy. Zacchaeus was one of his friends.
ALL: We thank you, God, for Jesus.
CHILDREN: Jesus was forgiving. As he died he prayed for the people who killed him.
ALL: We thank you, God, for Jesus.
CHILDREN: Jesus was loving. He blessed little children.
ALL: We thank you, God, for Jesus.
CHILDREN: Jesus went about doing good. He cared for the sick, the hungry, and the sad. He always helped people.
ALL: We thank you, God, for Jesus.
PARENTS: Jesus showed us what God is like. He showed us how to live with one another. Let us remember Jesus and give thanks for him.
ALL: We thank you, God, for Jesus.

Assignment: Read the entire Gospel of Mark to come to know the whole story of the life of Jesus. Assume that many people really do not know the story.

Session 2 Theme: Enemies of Jesus

(On the bulletin board, or in some prominent place, have the question: "If Jesus was so good how come he was killed?")

As group arrives hand out scripts to "Monday" from Journey With Jesus Through Holy Week by Judy Gattis Smith, published by Contemporary Drama Service.

On work tables are paper plates and felt-tipped markers. All persons are instructed to draw a face on the paper plates. One side of the plate should have a happy face, the opposite side should have an angry face.

When the faces are completed the leader selects a person to read the part of Jesus in the playlet and assigns the various solo lines. Everyone else reads the chorus. The play is read without rehearsal or movement. Each person uses his mask, turning it from happy to angry at the appropriate times.

The following is an excerpt from <u>Journey With Jesus Through Holy Week</u>.

JOURNEY WITH JESUS THROUGH HOLY WEEK

CHORUS:	We are the sellers of pigeons. Come and trade with us.
SOLO I:	My pigeons are the whitest.
SOLO II:	My pigeons fly the highest.
CHORUS:	A pigeon for a sacrifice. You can buy it here.
SOLO I:	Trade with me, I charge you less.
SOLO II:	Trade with <u>me</u>, I serve you best.
CHORUS:	Listen to the hustle and bustle. Let us bargain with you.
SOLO I:	Will you pay a denarius for a pigeon?
SOLO II:	No? Then what's my best offer?
CHORUS:	Win God's favor. Offer our pigeons for sacrifice.
JESUS:	NO! You cannot use the temple for a marketplace! This is a house of prayer. I will upset your seats and open your cages. You make our Temple a den of thieves.
CHORUS:	*(Turning masks to frowning sides)* Our pigeons! Our profits! They are getting away.
SOLO I:	They are flying free.
SOLO II:	Try to catch them.
SOLO I:	They are out of reach.
CHORUS:	Our stools are broken. Our cages shattered. *(Slower)* We will get even with you, Jesus of Nazareth. *(Small pause — then masks turn to smiling side)*

Following the session list the enemies of Jesus named in the play.

We do not want children to feel hatred for the people who killed Jesus. We want to help them gain some understanding of *why* the people did it and of Jesus' attitude toward them.

Jesus had powerful and important people as enemies. What was it they feared from him?

Questions to be discussed in small groups or as a whole:

1. Is it true that whenever a person is really honest and courageous he makes enemies of dishonest people? Why?

2. Is it worth being good if being good gets you into serious trouble? Why?

The most awful thing in the death of Jesus is that it was brought about by men who were following or believed themselves to be following good and honorable reasons for their actions. Men of various classes united to crucify Jesus. Men like you and me.

Assignment: Families continue reading the Book of Mark at home.

Assign parts to the play The Sycamore Perspective. Encourage the chosen actors, a family if possible, to practice at home.

Session 3 Theme: Forgiveness and Salvation

Chairs are assembled in a semi-circle with a stage area. Persons performing The Sycamore Perspective sit together on chairs in the stage area.

The play, dealing with forgiveness and salvation, is presented. Following is an excerpt from The Sycamore Perspective by Julie Marlin, published by Contemporary Drama Service.

THE SYCAMORE PERSPECTIVE

ZACCHAEUS: You mean poor people like lepers have been climbing this tree?

BIRD: Don't worry Zack, the lepers can't get up to the branch you are on. So tell me Zack, what brings you up here?

ZACCHAEUS: I want to see who this Jesus is. All those people out there are crowded around waiting for him. I know he will come this way sometime, and when he does, I want to get a good look at him.

BIRD: You will have a birdseye view from that branch.

ZACCHAEUS: *(After looking over crowd)* So, who is this Jesus? *(Interrupting his own question)* Aha! Look at that!

BIRD: What?

ZACCHAEUS: . . . that bald head!

BIRD: That's not Jesus.

ZACCHAEUS: Who? Oh, yes, yes, of course that is not Jesus. That is
Hal! Hal, tall Hal is the old buzzard who calls me bald.
Now that I can see the top of his head he is as bald as
a hen's egg. And he calls me "Baldy"! All this time he
has been looking down on my thinning pate and making
fun of the very thing on me, that is wrong with him!

BIRD: It's like they always say, "takes one to know one."

ZACCHAEUS: Keep your wise quacks to yourself, Shorty.

BIRD: *(To himself)* Like they always say . . .

ZACCHAEUS: Now there is a ridiculous spectacle. That little short
guy down there stretching and bending in hopeless
contortions to see over the crowd. *(To person in the
crowd)* Why don't you give up, Shorty! If the good
Lord had meant for you to see over the crowd he'd
have given you longer legs!

BIRD: That is very profound. Did you make that up yourself?

ZACCHAEUS: You know, Bird, this is a whole new world up here.
When I stood on the ground all that I ever saw were
purses and belts, belts and purses, and more purses. My
whole life was absorbed in purses. I never knew there
was so much to see. This tree is wonderful!

Questions for discussion:

1. Have you ever been in a situation where you were mistreated and
you responded by trying to "get even"? What was the result?

2. Has anyone ever forgiven you for something you did wrong?
What was the result?

3. Has anyone a story to tell about the joy it is to know that God
forgives us — about how Jesus makes us new by saving us from
doubt and fear?

4. Read aloud John 12:12-19 and Mark 15:6-20. Do you think one
person could have been in both crowds? Have you ever had an
experience where you were nice to a person one day and mean
the next or vice versa?

If time permits create a greeting card for someone you have forgiven or asked for forgiveness. Or create a card that celebrates someone else's discovery of the power of Jesus, as a saving part of their life.

Send the card.

Session 4 Theme: Death

Children are able to consider, talk about and question death from a young age. They are likely to have had some direct experience with death of persons or animals. During the Easter season children hear about the death of Jesus. This gives rise to many questions that adults should try to answer.

As persons arrive assign parts of Owl, Lion, Eagle, Butterfly and Flower from the play Death and Dying — I'm Not Afraid Now by Judy Gattis Smith.

Spend a few moments at the beginning of the session creating costumes for these characters and dressing them. Have on hand supplies of newspapers and scissors and tape, crepe paper in appropriate colors, feathers, pipe cleaners, etc.

Present the play Death and Dying — I'm Not Afraid Now, published by Contemporary Drama Service. Excerpt follows:

DEATH AND DYING — I'M NOT AFRAID NOW

ANDY: Who are you and what are you doing here?

LION: Don't you recognize a lion when you see one? Maybe this will help. (Lion gets down on all fours and roars)

ANDY: Okay, Okay, I believe you. But what are you doing here?

LION: I came to help you with that question about fear. Haven't you ever heard that a lion is the bravest of all animals? Fear questions are my department.

ANDY: I'm standing here talking to an owl and a lion. Weird!

LION: Do you want an answer or don't you?

ANDY: Okay, okay.

LION: Here it is: We're all afraid of something we've never done before.

ANDY: That's it? That's my answer?

LION: Look at it this way. Are you afraid to go into a dark room alone?

ANDY: Yes!

LION: Are you afraid to go out at night into a dark woods alone?

ANDY: Yes!

LION: But — would you be afraid if your father were holding your hand?

ANDY: No.

LION: It's the same way with death. God is our Father and he goes right there with us and holds our hand. We don't need to be afraid because we trust Him.

ANDY: *(Excited)* Hey! I see what you mean!

OWL: Any more questions?

A suggested question and answer period is included in this playkit which gives children an opportunity to respond to the questions posed by Andy in the play and to ask questions of their own on this subject. Your minister might be invited to this particular session to guide the group in your church's understanding of death.

Assignment: Assign parts to the play This Do In Remembrance Of Me, to be presented next week.

Session 5 Theme: Maundy Thursday

Leader: Today we come together to think about Maundy Thursday, a special day of remembrance.

The whole life of the church has dwindled to its lowest pulse on Maundy Thursday. We are just before the catastrophe of Good Friday.

Let's listen to the story. Use your imagination and put yourself into the scene.

Do the play This Do In Remembrance Of Me, by Carol Dulmes, published by Contemporary Drama Service. Excerpt follows on pg. 89.

JOHN: Easy man. Next we'll need the healing hand of the Master for you. I understand how you feel. I, too, would defend him. *(Pause)* There seems to be something on his mind lately . . . that and the way he draws us aside so often to tell us about the kingdom . . . and the Father . . . I don't understand and yet I feel as if he is waiting for something . . . watching and waiting . . . and preparing us for it.

PETER: Well, I am prepared tonight. With the mood in this city, I armed myself before I came. See. *(Draws a small dagger out of the folds of his cloak)*

JOHN: But, Peter, it is not lawful to . . .

PETER: Say nothing. I hear them on the stairs. *(Jesus and the rest of the disciples enter. Matthew carries the lamb and James has some unleavened bread.)*

JESUS: Peace be to you, Peter and John. Are all things ready?

PETER: Shalom, Master. We have found the room as you said and everything is ready according to the law.

JOHN: Welcome, Lord. Peace be to you, my brethren.

MATTHEW: Here, Peter. The woman sent the lamb up with me. See how well roasted it is? And me, as hungry as a lion of Judah.

JAMES: You are always hungry, Matthew. I can see why you took up tax collecting before. They eat well, no? Here John. Martha sent along some more unleavened bread. She wanted to be sure we had enough and Mary sent us her love and best wishes. *(John takes it and thanks them)*

PETER: Everything is ready, Master. Will you take your place at the center? John, you next to him . . . Judas, next to John . . . James *(He gestures for them all)* . . . Simon. . . Andrew . . . Thomas . . . Matthew, over here close to the roast . . . the other James . . . Philip and Bartholomew, on the end here . . . Thaddaeus, next . . . do we have enough places? Good. I'll sit here next to Jesus.

JUDAS: *(Aside)* I thought that's what he had in mind.

JESUS: I have been looking forward to this supper with you with all of my being. It will be the last time we are together before my suffering and death. *(Peter catches John's eye and pats his robe where the dagger is hidden)* In truth, I tell you I will not eat anymore until the kingdom of God is fulfilled.

Following the play the group creates a mobile to help us remember. Idea and art work are by Judy Wood.

The following is a drawing of the mobile.

A MOBILE
To help me remember...

SHELL:

Through baptism we become part of God's family.

CROSS:

Communion is a time to remember that Christ died for us.

BUTTERFLY:

Communion is a joyful sharing of Christ's resurrection.

GRAPES & BREAD:

Communion is receiving the body and blood of Christ and the forgiveness of our sins.

PEOPLE:

Communion is a fellowship of God's people.

JOY:

Communion is a joyful celebration by God's people.

Session 6 Theme: Easter!

Our final session brings us to Easter. It is the greatest and oldest of the Christian festivals, the "feast of feasts" as Pope Leo the Great called it early in the 5th century. Easter joy is more profound than smiles and laughter because of what it took to create it.

After the group has gathered the leader leads the group in the participation drama <u>Listen to Easter,</u> by Judy Gattis Smith, published by Contemporary Drama Service. All persons take part by creating the sound effects. Here is an excerpt.

LISTEN TO EASTER

(NOTE: Hold up cards cueing group sounds as indicated)

NARRATOR: As soon as you enter the garden you will hear it — the slow marching tread of the Roman soldiers. *(Sound Group I)* Two guards have been posted there all night. One marches now — back and forth — in measured tread, before a sealed tomb. *(Sound Group I)*

A still starry darkness fills the sky. There is a strange silence with the occasional murmur of a soft mournful wind. *(Sound Group II)*

If you listen very carefully you can hear another sound — the soft weeping of Jesus' heartbroken followers. *(Sound Group III)* Their hope, their joy is gone and they are left with numb emptiness. Their Lord is dead! *(Sound Group III)*

The older soldier who is not marching now but resting, hears all these sounds — the marching footsteps *(Sound Group I)*, the soft wind *(Sound Group II)*, and the distant weeping *(Sound Group III)*. But these sounds are drowned out by a louder sound that echoes in his memory — the sound of the mob before the crucifixion *(Sound Group IV)*. He cannot shake the memory of this strange day. He listens again to the wind *(Sound Group II)* and remembers the eerie stillness and dark pall of the sun following the crucifixion and the loud crack of thunder that echoed across the valley and died slowly in the distance. He listens to the weeping *(Sound Group III)* and remembers the faces of the few women crowding around the cross and the small handful of men who were followers. He hears again the cries of the mob *(Sound Group IV)* and remembers their anger and their excitement. He listens to the footsteps *(Sound Group I)* and wonders why they must guard, for three days, a tomb that is blocked with an unmovable stone that no two men could budge and sealed over tightly with the seal of Caesar.

Leader: The message of Easter is this — He lives! He has the Power to change life. There was a power released at Easter that withstood emperors and empires — that created the New Testament — that began the Christian church. It is a Power that has never been completely fathomed and never will be. It is the Power of God made known in Jesus. That is the meaning of Easter.

As a closing activity the entire group can make the "He Is Risen" banner, available from Contemporary Drama Service, Kit #P557. Be sure to have on hand all needed material and supplies as suggested in the kit. The fabric is not included and must be purchased ahead of time.

The banner can then be carried by a procession into the church or it can be hung in a prominent place in your church or church school as a permanent reminder of the time when intergenerationally, you, as a class, lived out the moments that tell of the Easter story.

Outline of Entire Session: Plays and Projects

Session 1:   We Know About You Jesus with slides. Responsive readings. Write a prayer.

Session 2:   Journey with Jesus Through Holy Week. Make masks. Discuss questions.

Session 3:   The Sycamore Perspective. Discussion questions. Make a greeting card.

Session 4:   Death and Dying — I'm Not Afraid Now. Make costumes. Discuss questions.

Session 5: <u>This Do In Remembrance of Me</u>. Make a remembrance mobile.

Session 6: <u>Listen to Easter</u>. Make the "He Is Risen" banner.

This chapter uses resources available from Contemporary Drama Service to focus the themes of Lent and Easter. You may substitute other plays on these same themes. Look for plays that can be read in Reader's Theatre style — plays that can be assigned one week, taken home to practice and then be presented without rehearsal. Of course you can also use plays without sets or props or elaborate costumes.

APRIL:

Movement & Liturgical Dance

April is a month of movement. Can't you feel it in Nature? Jonquils, tulips, daffodils are pushing up from the ground. Brooks are set free with a tinkling ring and surging motions. Little clouds are moved by April winds. Even the sun seems to come dancing across the sky.

Eastertide, in our churches (not just Easter Sunday but the entire season) should express a dynamic, active life and growth. We rise from our knees before the cross and move back into life. Joy is the keynote of our Easter faith and singing and dancing are a by-product of joy.

A project of your drama group for April could appropriately be to bring movement and dance into your sanctuary worship.

We certainly have Biblical sanction, for example:

Psalm 149:3 — Let them praise His name with dancing.
II Samuel 6:14 — And King David danced before God
with all his might.
Psalm 150 — Praise Him with timbrel and dance.

While we know from the Bible that dance has always been a method of worshipping it has been de-emphasized. Reinstating it in your congregation can be an exciting challenge.

Movement and dance, under the sponsorship of your drama group could take three forms:

1. The congregation can be involved in movement.
2. Children of the congregation can be dancers.
3. Liturgical dance can be performed.

Let's begin with simple movements of the congregation.

A leader might say something like the following to the congregation:

"You have worshipped God with your voices using hymns, prayers and responsive readings. Your intellect and thoughts have been involved. Now let's praise him with motion, grace and physical strength."

You might begin with simple movements. Members of the congregation can lift arms upward to God. It is an interesting experience to read the Scripture of Moses on Mt. Ararat. When his arms were uplifted the Israelites won. When they were down the battle went against them. Following the Biblical reading the congregation can lift their arms as the pastor leads in prayer. I Timothy 2:3 "I will therefore that men pray everywhere lifting up holy hands."

Another simple movement for a congregation is touching fingertips. From birth on, our hands set us apart from other animals. As a mother holds her newborn child for the first time she looks in wonderment at the beauty of his perfectly shaped hand. As the father bends down to the newborn child, he marvels at the determination of the baby's grip on his finger.

Luke 5:13 "Jesus touched him and he was healed." Many of the stories in the Gospels of Jesus' healing ministry can be read, followed by fingertip touching of members of the congregation.

Other movements with the hands can be meaningful. During the period of prayer palms can be down upon a person's knees as they pray to drain bad habits and thoughts from their lives, then turned upward to receive the gifts of God's love and strength.

Reaching out and swaying are two other very simple movements that can involve a congregation in a meaningful way. All of these can be done with persons standing or sitting at their place.

Look at hymns and scripture used in your congregational worship and see if you can incorporate directions for simple participating movement. Some examples of directions in which to move are: up, down, back and forth, backward, forward, across, sideways, the other way, over, under, above, below, in a circle, underneath, beneath, between, to the side of, to the other side of, to the back of, and to the front of.

Jumping is an interesting movement. We've heard the expression "jump for joy". Yet have you ever seen a congregation, seeking to express joy, jump? Jumping is also associated with impatience, curiosity and excitement and a desire of a child to get his own way. How can we incorporate this very natural means of self-expression into meaningful worship?

A child or experienced dancer might demonstrate a "jump for joy" down the aisle of your church. Begin on left foot. Give a short hop. Then a long leap forward with the right foot. Land on the right foot. Do a short recovery hop. Leap forward with left foot and repeat.

A common misconception is that the integration of body movement, gesture, etc. is possible only with the help of professional dancers. These very simple movements can help your congregation prepare for more involvement, using their bodies to express their feelings about God.

A next step might be to have dancers invite the people of the congregation to follow their movements. A hymn, such as "For the Beauty of the Earth" could be used. The congregation is asked to stand. The dancers sing and interpret a line from the song with movements and then the congregation sings and echoes the same movements.

"For the Beauty of the Earth" — *Arms could swing out and down.*
"For the Glory of the Sky" — *Arms could swing upward, etc.*

The congregation is instructed to have their eyes follow their hands and keep the movements very slow. The movements should also be bigger than life.

These very simple movements become powerful for when you say something with creative movement you feel it within. Reassure your congregation that there is no right or wrong way to move. Express your feelings.

Your next step might be to introduce some easy steps in pews where some worshippers will feel safer. A left, right, left, hop; then right, left, right, hop to any lively hymn in 4/4 time could add a joyful dimension to your worship.

A congregation dancing is not a congregation expressing a dull drudgery type of worship. Look for the smiles! Look for the joy!

As shyness is overcome and this form of worship is accepted move the people out into the aisles. Circle the pews with persons joining hands and doing a simple step-skip-step, clockwise to hymns such as "This Is My Father's World".

Using children as dancers can bring appreciation and pleasure to a congregation.

Try a joyful Easter parade where children march and dance in single file behind a beautiful butterfly standard. A standard is like a processional cross except in this case it is a large, fanciful butterfly made with movable wings and flowing crepe paper streamers. Children imitating butterflies could follow close behind, dressed in costumes and blowing party favors (the kind that blow out and roll up) for butterfly feelers. What joy and vitality this would bring to a church service!

Music and movement come naturally to young children. Look for ways to allow them to sway, hop and skip to express joy to God. Use songs that include hand clapping and foot tapping.

As we watch children, moving with joy, we are reminded of the ancient Scripture: "The Lord takes pleasure in his people." Psalm 149:4

Perhaps your drama group would like to form or sponsor a liturgical dance or interpretive movement group.

This group would choreograph familiar hymns, Christmas carols, prayers, litanies and passages from scripture. These groups are often made up of youth but really need not be confined to any age level. Such a group would use the universal, basic language of symbolic movement to bring spiritual enrichment to the lives of others.

A beautiful by-product for those taking part in such a group is that the spiritual truths they are portraying saturate deep into their lives as they use the powerful dimension of symbolic movement. The body becomes not only a mirror but an instrument of the soul.

If the idea of creative movement is new to you, study pictures of varieties of movements that communicate meaning. Acquire an awareness of the many subtle ways in which, without saying a word, a person communicates meaning through his bodily movements.

Following are some ways in which to move: slowly, quietly, quickly, loudly, heavily, silently, hurriedly, sadly, happily, softly and joyfully.

The strength of dance over drama is that where drama is restricted to human or animal characters dancers can portray cosmic forces — the sea, light and dark, love, power, the vitality of flames, the fluidity of water.

Janet Litherland, in her introduction to Let's Move gives five important points for liturgical dancers to remember:

1. The purpose of liturgical dance is worship, not entertainment.
2. Intense concentration on the material being interpreted is essential to worship, both for the dancers and for the observers.
3. The face should express inner feelings — pain, happiness, distress, hope, etc.
4. Dancers do not sing or speak while interpreting. Material is presented by a singing or speaking choir, an ensemble, a soloist, an instrument, or a narrator.
5. Dancers must "warm up" with simple exercises before the rehearsal and before the service.

Ten liturgical dance interpretations are included in the Let's Move kit. These would be good starting movements to use both as a means of introducing liturgical dance into your congregational worship and as helpful resources for a group that would eventually wish to do its own choreography.

There are two liturgical dances for regular portions of most Protestant services: the Doxology and the Lord's Prayer. These interpretations done by a liturgical choir would make what may have become ritual, come alive. For example, the following excerpt from Let's Move by Janet Litherland, published by Contemporary Drama Service.

PRAISE GOD, FROM WHOM ALL BLESSINGS FLOW

Starting Position: Feet together; hands at sides; head bowed.

PRAISE GOD, FROM WHOM ALL BLESSINGS FLOW;
> Feet apart as arms swing up and out on GOD; arms slowly down
> at sides to waist level, sweeping out front on FLOW, palms up.

PRAISE HIM ALL CREATURES HERE BELOW;
> Both arms up right on PRAISE. Left arm moves slowly down
> and to the left, finishing on BELOW.

PRAISE HIM ABOVE, YE HEAVENLY HOST;
> Bend slightly forward at waist, arms moving together to the left;
> straighten the body as arms circle up and to the right; bend once
> again and continue circle, ending straight with arms up left.

PRAISE FATHER, SON, AND HOLY GHOST.
> Bend at waist, still facing slightly left, as arms are lowered and
> extended in back of body. Legs are straight, head bowed low.

AMEN.
> Straighten (still facing slightly left) and reach up left with both
> arms on AH; feet apart, arms up and out to sides on MEN.
> Focus up.

In addition creative movements are suggested for familiar Scripture
passages, well-known hymns and popular Spiritual songs.

Suggestions for costumes from <u>Let's Move</u> are: choir robes, sash at
waist, a mantle or stole secured across the shoulders, a long wrap
which entwines the waist and sweeps up to cover the head, leotards
and stockings covered by knee-length tunics, bare feet, stocking feet
or soft sandals.

"As the group matures in ability and dedication it will want to design
its own choreography. This is ideal, for the dance then becomes a true
expression of the dancer's own inner feelings. Create, concentrate and
worship!"

Dance is an expression of the whole being and wholeness is the essence
of Christianity — which calls for the devotion not of the mind alone
but of heart, soul and strength.

Another possibility for using movement would be to produce a musical. A musical story is a narrative that combines drama, music and
movement. It may have music throughout or used just as a theme that
comes at the start or finish of the story.

At first all acting was done in the orchestra and the chorus was most important. It danced and chanted or sang a commentary on the performance of the actors. Movement might be added to a production that calls for a chorus. Dancing breaks the monotony of dialogue and action and brings lightness and color. It can serve to stir the imagination and enhance aesthetic appreciation.

Some musicals available from Contemporary Drama Service are:

The Return, book and lyrics by James C. Huffstutler, music by Howard E. Dexter and The Washbasin, also by James C. Huffstutler.

Jonah, words and music by Virginia Egermeier.

MAY:

One-Act Plays
Monologues, Spontaneous Dramas on Family Values

May is a gentle month. May is a sentimental month. May is a soft month. Children go out-of-doors without their coats. Flowering trees, apple blossoms literally float their blossoms through the air.

A new attitude pervades our church. We have struggled through Lent and rejoiced with Easter. Now we, like the fragrant blossoms move gently through Eastertide. We walk the Emmaus Road. And if our faith journey is true we become more sensitive to the living presence of the risen Christ around us. We begin to prepare ourselves to receive the gift of the Holy Spirit at Pentecost.

The image of Jesus as the Good Shepherd has meaning for us in May. We can say with conviction, "He leads me beside still waters."

And yet, though our Liturgical Year should help us identify the feelings within us and give us strength and support, this gentle month can be a month of frustration in our church.

School is ending and our students are under pressure to finish papers, excel at tests, complete projects. There is the feeling we must end things with a bang — that somehow we have failed if things end gently, if they float to completion.

And May does bring a sense of things completed. May seems to be a ribbon that wraps up a portion of the year.

Your drama group may feel that they want to end the school year with a grand production. Better to go with the flow. The Youth Group which is winding up their school year may be the best group to produce a drama this month.

A sentimental production like The Velveteen Rabbit (available for a cast of four from Contemporary Drama Service) could be the program for a Mother's Day dinner or a program to conclude your year's work. The script can be read in the style of Reader's Theatre or memorized and presented in a modified theatrical style. This classic by Margery Williams, which speaks to all ages could be given for children as they wind up a portion of the Church School year. Following is an excerpt from The Velveteen Rabbit.

THE VELVETEEN RABBIT

FOUR: The Skin Horse had lived longer in the nursery than any of the others. He was so old that his brown coat was bald in patches and showed the seams underneath, and most of the hairs in his tail had been pulled out to string bead necklaces. He was wise, for he had seen a long succession of mechanical toys arrive to boast and swagger, and by-and-by break their mainsprings and pass away, and he knew that they were only toys, and would never turn into anything else. *(Slight pause)* For nursery magic is very strange and wonderful, and only those playthings that are old and wise and experienced, like the Skin Horse, understand all about it. *(Moving toward CS)* One day, when they were laying side by side near the nursery fender, before Nana came to tidy the room, the little Rabbit asked . . .

TWO: What is Real? Does it mean having things that buzz inside you and a stick-out handle?

ONE: Real isn't how you're made, it's a thing that happens to you. When a child loves you for a long, long time, not just to play with, but really loves you, then you become Real.

TWO: Does it hurt?

ONE: Sometimes.

FOUR: *(Aside)* The Skin Horse was always truthful.

ONE: But when you're Real, you don't mind being hurt.

TWO: Does it happen all at once, like being wound up, or bit by bit?

ONE: No, it doesn't happen all at once. You become! And it takes a long time. That's why it doesn't often happen to people who break easily, or who have sharp edges, and have to be carefully kept. Generally, by the time you are Real, most of your hair has been loved off, and your eyes drop out and you get loose in the joints and very shabby. But these things don't matter at all, because once you are real you can't be ugly, except to people who don't understand.

THE VELVETEEN RABBIT *(contd)*

TWO: I suppose <u>you</u> are Real?

FOUR: *(Aside)* Said the Rabbit. And then he wished he had not said it, for he thought the Skin Horse might be sensitive. But the Skin Horse only smiled.

ONE: The Child's Uncle made me Real. And that was a great many years ago. But once you are Real you can't become unreal again. It lasts for always.

FOUR: The Rabbit sighed. He thought it would be a long time before this magic called Real happened to him.

TWO: *(Stepping forward into Narrative Persona)* He longed to become Real, to know what it felt like; and yet the idea of growing shabby and losing his eyes and whiskers was rather sad. He wished that he could become it without these uncomfortable things happening to him.

Mother's Day can be experienced in our church school with monologues for women. A number of these are available from Contemporary Drama Service: The Women Speak; The Matchless Marys; Five Women; or Beautiful Within. The beauty of presenting these in May is not only to celebrate Mother's Day but because this method of drama is in tune with the season. A monologue does not necessitate juggling busy schedules to find rehearsal time. A woman will prepare her presentation on her own time. A soft draping of a headdress suggests the mood of another day — another time. You might want to study these available monologues and then write your own.

Persons in your congregation can do a beautiful job of writing their own monologues. The assignment was given at a workshop at The Presbyterian School of Christian Education, Richmond, VA, to read the story of Jesus on the Emmaus Road and write a monologue.

Following is an example of one of those original monologues by Donald E. Howard. A note from Mr. Howard: "Just as a word of explanation as to how I came up with this monologue. For several years I directed a choir and became interested in the development of liturgy, especially the offices (martins, vespers, etc.). When we were given the passage from Luke, I noticed Verse 29 is one of the opening sentences of the vesper service. So I decided to cast the monologue as an imaginary explanation of how this verse might have become part of the tradition which developed in the early church."

"John, bring the children to me. *(Pause)*
No, I'm not too tired. I can rest later. I must speak to them now. *(Pause)*
Ah children, come here to grandpa. I want to talk with you. Did you say
    your prayers before supper this evening? Hmm? What did you say?
    (Pause) And then what? *(Pause)* That's right. "Stay with me, Lord,
    for it is evening and the day is almost over."

Do you know why we say that prayer in our home? *(Pause)* Let me tell
    you a story.
When I was a young man — about your father's age, Mary, our Lord was
    still alive. But the priests and rulers conspired with the Romans to
    have him killed. Do you know that story? *(Pause)*
Well, on the third day after he was crucified I was walking back to
    Emmaus from Jerusalem with my friend Simon. We were stopped
    by a stranger. He asked us why we were so sorrowful. We couldn't
    believe that he hadn't heard what had happened, so we explained
    how they had crucified our Lord, and now the women were say-
    ing that his body was missing from the tomb. *(Pause)*
Yes, James, the stranger was Jesus, but we didn't know that yet. We
    didn't recognize him.

Then he began to walk with us, and he told us about the prophecies.
    Oh, he talked until we reached home. When he started to leave I
    said to him, "Stay with us. It's evening. The day is almost over."
So we went inside and your grandmother fixed us something to eat.
    When we sat down the stranger took the bread, blessed it, and
    broke it. And just like that we knew who he was. And the next
    instant he was gone. *(Pause)* No, no he just vanished. And suddenly
    we understood what he had said to us as we were walking along
    the road.
Well, Simon and I jumped up and ran back to Jerusalem to tell the
    others that Jesus was alive — that we had seen him and talked with
    him.
After that day, every time I come to the table in the evening I am re-
    minded of when our risen Lord had been here. One day I thought:
    What if I had not invited him to stay. He might have gone on and
    we never would have seen that he had been raised from the dead.

So every evening I began to repeat those words, to ask the Lord to stay
    with us, to remind us that he is alive. *(Pause)*

You must go now. Grandpa is very tired and needs to rest. Will you
    remember this story? If you need to be reminded ask your mothers
    and fathers. They heard it many times as they were growing up.
And you must remember the story." *

*Permission to reprint the Emmaus Monologue was granted by Donald E. Howard.

Church School teachers grow weary in May. They sense the itching of the children to be outdoors — to be already in the routine of summer and they feel their own tinges of Spring fever. Vary your teaching routine with children by taking them outdoors this month. Use a participation story with them such as The Boyhood of Jesus where children listen to a story and then make the sound effects. Or, use this as a model and create your own participation stories from your Church School curriculum material. Following is an excerpt from The Boyhood of Jesus by Judy Gattis Smith, published by Contemporary Drama Service.

THE BOYHOOD OF JESUS

NARRATOR:

Now Jesus ran *(Running steps)*. He left the cultivated lands and approached the steeper hillsides around Nazareth. His feet skirted a wealth of wild flowers. He ran past fig trees decked in pale leaves and tiny fruit. The scarlet blossoms of pomegranate flashed by as he ran. "Oh, Father, how beautiful is your world" he sang as he ran *(Footsteps stop)*. A new sound came to Jesus — the quiet sound of sheep moving up the pasture field *(Sound)*. Then a frightening sound — the call of a wolf *(Sound)*. Jesus did not like the wolf. For him it was a symbol of treachery. From his vantage point atop the hill, he could not see the large grey form and as he listened the call grew more distant *(Sound)*. The gentle flock of sheep with coats of brown and black and white meandered slowly up the hill *(Sound)*. Jesus spotted the shepherd. He recognized him as a man from the village; a good shepherd who would give his life for his sheep and not a hireling who would flee at the approach of a wolf. A lamb balked. The shepherd picked it up and carried it on his shoulders. Jesus smiled.

It was time for him to return now. Among the common people one had to work hard at an early age and already Jesus' household would be stirring.

Before returning he remembered all the sounds he had heard: the rooster *(Sound)*, the donkey *(Sound)*, the wind in the barley *(Sound)*, the turtledove *(Sound)*, the wolf *(Sound)* and the sheep *(Sound)* and he thanked God for the beauty and excitement of His world. Then, with heart overflowing, Jesus' day began.

Copyright ©MCMLXXII Meriwether Publishing Ltd./Contemporary Drama Service Box 7710, Colorado Springs, CO 80933.

May is associated with Family Month in many of our churches.

Another possibility for use of drama in May calls for dealing with some of the serious questions raised and problems posed by living together as a family. Your drama group (or one of your adult Sunday School classes) may wish to sponsor an evening of clarifying values in a family through the use of spontaneous drama. Following is a suggested outline for such an evening. This program can be used intergenerationally. Each skit involves twelve to fifteen persons so a large group of fifty to sixty persons would be necessary to create this program.

Introduction (by Leader for the evening):

Teaching values has always been an important part of Christian education. Usually this has taken the form of moralizing. Dr. Sidney Simon and his colleagues have brought to our attention another way of teaching values. (Values Clarification by Simon, Howe and Kirschenbaum, Hart Publishing Co., 1972 and Meeting Yourself Halfway, Simon, Argus Communications, 1974.) This process, called value clarification, says there are many diverse, alternative values in our society and the decision and responsibility for making choices in values lies squarely with each individual.

One way Dr. Simon suggests clarifying our values is through looking at alternative possibilities in a situation and choosing priorities. There are no clear cut right or wrong answers. Each individual must choose.

This idea is the basis for the following skits. In each there is a situation and three possible solutions. Actors are to understand the problem situation and then they are assigned one of the three solutions to act out spontaneously. Discussion of what happened and why follows the skits. Students become aware of how a person in that situation might feel and act and thus clarify their own feelings and values.

OUTLINE

1. Opening. Welcome all persons. Introduce topic. If needed include some input on intergenerational study.

2. Explain procedure for spontaneous drama. If you would feel more secure some persons might be contacted before the session and told they would be chosen for roles. However — no rehearsing nor any coaching!

3. Present, spontaneously, one or more skits.

4. Whole group discusses the questions. Or, divide into small groups of six to eight persons for discussions.

5. If time permits, respond creatively to the topic presented in the skit.

Situation 1: Grandmother's Case (for ages 8 through adult)

Three families are seated around three dinner tables. Twelve actors come forward creating three scenes. You may use real props or imaginary ones.

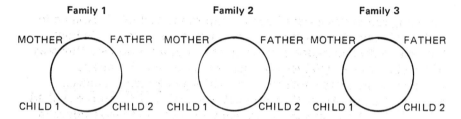

Problem Situation: Grandmother, who has always been independent, is getting old and somewhat senile. The family must make a decision about what to do about her. Families are all average families, typical of your community.

Family 1: Decides to put her in a nursing home nearby. Father announces this to the family and they discuss the pros and cons.

Family 2: Decides to provide a small apartment for her. Mother announces this to the family and they discuss the pros and cons.

Family 3: Decides to take her into their own home. Father announces this to the family and they discuss the pros and cons.

Instructions to Actors: Think about your roles. Children decide on your age and sex. Try to actually get into your character and express yourself as your character would.

Instructions to Leader: As director of this skit you begin the action after the characters have had time to think about their role. Begin with any of the three families. After they have established their solution and when it seems appropriate, "cut" to the next family. Do not allow the situations to bog down. It may also be necessary for you to remind the actors to "stay in character". You will set the tone for the skit by your seriousness. When the three families have role-played their situation, introduce Scene 2.

SCENE 2: Grandmother hears about the situation and is extremely unhappy with the solution. (Choose three more actors to be "Grandmother" in each situation.) Grandmother comes to the family in tears about the situation. Why is she so unhappy with this solution and what happens now?

Act out the situation spontaneously as you did for Scene 1. Family members will remain in the same parts.

SCENE 3: It is the most important part of the role-play because here the actors and the audience must make their decision or at least begin to understand the values they would prize in this particular situation. The Leader asks these questions:

1. Were the characters believable? (As Leader do not allow comments on the acting ability of the players but emphasize the believability of the persons — would persons in that situation react in that manner?)

2. Which of the three solutions would you choose and why?

3. Do you know of persons who have been in a similar situation?

4. Would anyone offer a fourth solution?

Situation 2: The Divorce Case (for ages 8 through adult)

There are nine players in Scene 1: three children in three families. The children are sitting together in the living room. You may use real props or imaginary ones. Family 1 is a low-income family, Family 2 is a middle-class family and Family 3 is a high-income family.

SCENE 1:

CHILD 1	CHILD 1	CHILD 1
CHILD 2 CHILD 3	CHILD 2 CHILD 3	CHILD 2 CHILD 3
Family 1	Family 2	Family 3

Problem Situation: Your mother and father do not get along. They have had problems for several years and it has now reached the crisis stage. There has been no violence or unusual cruelty — just what the courts would call "irreconcilable differences". They have told you that they will decide something this afternoon and let you know. The children are discussing together their situation, how they feel about it, and what it has been like for them and what solutions they can suggest.

Instructions to Actors: Think about your role. Decide on your age and sex. Try to project to the audience your family's economic level.

Instructions to Leader: This first scene will probably be short for each family. Try to let each scene run until the children have established, in some way, their economic level and their individual feelings. Begin with any of the three families and "cut" to the next when it seems appropriate. When the three families have role-played their situation, introduce Scene 2.

SCENE 2: Choose three more characters to play Mother or Father in each family. The parent comes in with the decision. The children and parent interact over the decision.

Family 1: The parents have decided to separate and each keep the children for part of the year.

Family 2: The parents have decided to stay together for the sake of the children even though it means unhappiness for each of them.

Family 3: The parents have decided to begin legal actions for a divorce.

Act out the situation spontaneously as you did for Scene 1. The children of the three families will remain in the same parts.

SCENE 3: Discussion of the situation.

1.   Do we have stereotyped ideas of how people in different social levels will react? Might each of the three solutions be possible in any status? Why or why not?

2.   Were the characters believable? Were the ways they showed their economic level stereotyped?

3. If your parents were unhappily married which solution would you want them to take?

Situation 3: The Unemployed Father (for ages 8 through adult)

There are nine players in Scene 1: a mother and two children in three families. Each family is an average family from your community. The families are sitting together in the living room. You may use real props or imaginary ones.

SCENE 1:

CHILD 1 CHILD 2	CHILD 1 CHILD 2	CHILD 1 CHILD 2
MOTHER	MOTHER	MOTHER
Family 1	**Family 2**	**Family 3**

Problem Situation: After being out of work for some time, the father of the household has just been offered three jobs: a janitor in the public school for $300 a week, no chance of advancement; a job firing a furnace in a steel plant with long working hours and $400 a week; and a job greeting visitors at a tourist site for $200 a week. He has gone to interview for the jobs and decide which to accept. The families are discussing together their situation, how they have adjusted (or not adjusted) to the unemployment. Which job they hope he will accept and why.

Instructions to Actors: Think about your role. Children decide on your age and sex. Try to actually get into your character and express yourself as your character would.

Instructions to Leader: Begin with any of the three families. Let the scene run until the actors have established their identity and feelings about unemployment. "Cut" to the next family when the scene begins to bog down.

This first scene should be fairly short, just setting the mood for the father's return. Choose three more actors for "father" in Scene 2.

SCENE 2: The father returns with his decision.

Family 1: Father has chosen the job of janitor in the public school for $300 a week, no chance of advancement.

Family 2: Father has chosen the job of firing a furnace in a steel plant for $400 a week.

Family 3: Father has chosen the job of greeting visitors at a tourist site for $200 a week.

The father comes into the family circle and tells them his decision and the reasons for his choice. They respond, acting out spontaneously their feelings.

SCENE 3: A discussion of the situation.

1. Were the reasons given by the father believable?

2. Comment on the family's reaction. Was it believable?

3. Which job would you have chosen or wanted your father to choose?

4. What factors do you consider most important in choosing a job?

Situation 4: The Engaged Couple (for teenagers and adults)

This situation involves nine players in three situations in one scene. The scene is a Minister's study. The minister sits on one side of his desk, a young man and a young woman sit on the other side. You may use real props or imaginary ones.

STUDY 1	STUDY 2	STUDY 3
◯ MINISTER	◯ MINISTER	◯ MINISTER
◯ ◯	◯ ◯	◯ ◯
BOY GIRL	BOY GIRL	BOY GIRL

Problem Situation: This young couple has just become engaged. Both have finished school and have good jobs. They are counseling with their minister regarding their future plans and life styles.

Couple 1: Has decided that both will continue with their full-time jobs and share the housework.

Couple 2: Has decided that the wife will give up her job to keep house and raise a family.

Couple 3: Has decided that the husband will give up his job to keep house so the wife can pursue her career.

The minister discusses the situation with the couple. The couple tells the minister why they think their decision is best. The minister suggests problems they will face because of their decision.

Instructions to Actors: Acting couples should think of all the reasons they can to support their particular choice. Do your best to convince not only the minister, but the audience as well. Ministers should try to discourage the couple from their particular choice.

Instructions to Leader: Since this situation is only one scene your job will be to be sure the actors understand their assignments and begin the action. After the scene lead the audience in discussion.

DISCUSSION OF THE SITUATION:

1. Were the actors believable? Did the reasons they gave make sense?

2. Is there any one life style for all couples?

3. With which couple would you agree?

Depending on the number of persons attending, you may want to divide into small groups across intergenerational lines for the discussion questions following each skit.

One or more skits may be used for each session. It would be best not to use any more than three at one time.

If time allows you may want to follow the skit and discussion with a creative activity which gives everyone a chance to express their feelings on the particular topic. Learning is reinforced as students respond creatively to what they have learned. Some methods you may use for this are: fingerpainting, montage, clay modeling, drawing, cinquain poems, haiku poems, watercolors, and yarn pictures. These creative activities are the means by which persons can express their own personal affirmations of what they think, feel and value. It supplements the same kind of thing they will be doing through drama and discussion.

JUNE:

Drama Beyond Church Walls

Sidewalk Drama, Hotch-Potch Plays, Clowns, Community Parades, Drama as Social Agent

June comes with long, green weeks that seem endless to a child or a teacher. School is out, the grueling routine is set aside. There seems to be more time to spend. Children are eager to dress up and enthusiastic to play make-believe. Adults and youth are anxious to move outdoors, to expand into the community. What shall be the direction of our drama group this month? It's a month for sidewalk drama, for clowns, for moving into the community, for looking at drama as a means of community service. The outdoors calls us. There is a freshness. It is not yet too hot. In many churches the traditional church school year ends in June with the ending of public school.

Let's celebrate the event with a sidewalk celebration for children. Assemble your entire elementary Church School students and teachers. Choose six adult leaders from your drama group to tell teachings of Jesus and supervise drawings. Decide on the place for the service, either a sidewalk or a parking lot. Divide your space into six large sections not too close together. Assemble a complete set of pastel chalk for each square.

Leader begins: We are here today for a sidewalk celebration. *

The life of Jesus is the focus of this celebration; his person, his life, his teachings are our inspiration. Through the Bible we learn about the life he lived. We enter the world of Galilee, the lakeside, the hilltop. We walk with him along dusty trails and grassy slopes. Jesus told many stories during his life, and we want to remember and learn from these stories. We will divide into six groups. Each group has a corresponding number on one of the large squares on the sidewalk (or parking lot). In just a moment you will go to your correct square. When you get there a leader will tell you one of the teachings of Jesus and then your whole group will illustrate it with pastel chalk in your square on the sidewalk. When we have all finished we will gather again here and then we will form a procession and visit all of the squares, seeing and hearing again the wonderful stories of Jesus.

(Children go to groups. Member of the drama group tells the story and the group talks about what it means and how they will illustrate it.)*

Square 1: <u>The Sower</u> *

A man went out to sow. As he scattered the seed in the field, some of
it fell along the path and birds came and ate it up. Some of it fell on
rocky ground where there is little soil. The seeds soon sprouted because
the soil wasn't deep. Then when the sun came up it burned the young
plants and because the roots had not grown enough, the plants soon
dried up. Some of the seed fell among thorns which grew up and
choked the plants and they didn't bear grain. But some seeds fell in
good soil and the plants sprouted, grew, and bore grain, some had
thirty grains, others sixty and others one hundred. (Mark 4:3-8)

Square 2: <u>The Two House Builders</u>*

A wise man built his house on a rock. The rain poured down, the
rivers flooded over and the winds blew hard against the house. But it
did not fall, because it had been built on the rocks. But everyone who
hears these words of mine and does not obey them will be like a foolish man who built his house on the sand. The rain poured down, the
rivers flooded over, the winds blew hard against that house and it fell.
What a terrible fall that was! (Matthew 7:24-27)

Square 3: <u>Mustard Seed</u> *

The kingdom of God is like a mustard seed, the smallest seed in the
world. A man takes it and plants it in the ground. After a while it
grows up and becomes the biggest of all plants. It puts out such large
branches that the birds come and make their nests in its shade.
(Mark 4:31-32)

Square 4: <u>A Tree and Its Fruit</u> *

A healthy tree does not bear bad fruit, nor does a poor tree bear good
fruit. Every tree is known by the fruit it bears. You do not pick figs
from thorn bushes or gather grapes from bramble bushes. A good man
brings good out of the treasure of good things in his heart; a bad man
brings bad out of his treasure of bad things. For a man's mouth speaks
what his heart is full of. (Luke 6:43-45)

Square 5: <u>Light of the World</u> *

You are like light for the whole world. A city built on a hill cannot
be hid. Nobody lights a lamp to put it under a bowl. Instead, he puts

* Also part of <u>Sidewalk Celebration</u> publication. See footnote, page 121.

it on the lampstand where it gives light for everyone in the house. In the same way your light must shine before people, so that they will see the good things you do and give praise to your Father in Heaven. (Matthew 5:14-17)

Square 6: <u>Lilies of the Field</u>*

Do not be worried about the food and drink you need to stay alive, or about the clothes for your body. After all, isn't life worth more than food? And isn't the body worth more than clothes? Look at the birds flying around. They do not plant seeds, gather a harvest and put it in barns. Your Father in Heaven takes care of them. And why worry about clothes? Look how the wild flowers grow. They do not work or make clothes for themselves. But I tell you that not even Solomon, as rich as he was, had clothes as beautiful as one of these flowers. (Luke 12:22-28)

<u>Regathering Time</u>*

Leader: Let's all form a single file now, holding hands and we will process to the squares to hear the teachings of Jesus.

(Group sings one verse of "Tell Me The Stories Of Jesus" ** as they walk to the first square. They form a circle around the picture. Leader tells the story and explains the meaning and the illustration.)

Leader: *(Leads in Prayer)* Father, we thank you for this story of Jesus. Give us ears to hear and hearts to understand its meaning. Amen.

Continue to do this for six squares.*

You may choose other stories than those presented here. Be sure that your stories have strong visual images. Your group leader may choose to dramatize the story with pantomime or divide the story into parts and include other actors. Leave the chalk pictures on your sidewalk or parking lot as a witness to the community. The picture will stay on until the first rain. If you have a long sidewalk leading up to your church the bright pictures are a delightful surprise to persons attending church.

With this first step of moving drama into the community let's continue along these lines.

*Also part of <u>Sidewalk Celebration</u> publication. See footnote, page 121.

** From: The Methodist Hymnal, published by The Methodist Publishing House, Nashville, TN 1964. Used with permission.

Jesus was always walking endlessly. Should we not parade in his image and name? When Christ was on earth he called men to follow him and still does. There could be a parade of new members who have joined the church within the year. The minister reads their names (perhaps following a church service). They rise from their pews and join a parade moving out and around the church.

The entire congregation could parade to a hillside and sit there as someone from the drama group reads the Sermon on the Mount.

Another Biblical mountain story that has great dramatic possibilities is the story of Elijah and the prophets of Bael.

Father's Day comes in June. There could be a parade of family groups.

Some Biblical stories could be told simply and with impact as a parade. For example: let the congregation be the Children of Israel following Moses.

Read the stories of the procession to the Temple at Jerusalem in the time of Solomon and be that procession.

Parade through your town or community and end up at a picnic spot.

There is a beautiful custom in some of the smaller villages in England called "well-dressing". Dating back to the time when plagues were common, the villages which were spared the epidemic would decorate the community wells with living flower pictures of Biblical events as a thanksgiving to God. These scenes are as elaborate as some of our Rose Bowl parade floats yet done by local folk, not professionals. The skill, using only fresh flowers to create life-like scenes, has been passed down from generation to generation and is the project of an entire family.

When the scenes have been completed the village gathers at the community church. After a Service of Thanksgiving, the Priest, robed in his finest, moves out behind a cross bearer. The people join behind him and in solemn fashion they move from well to well, stopping for words of thanks from the Priest and giving all the people an opportunity to view these works.

Can your drama group think of a similar way to combine the flowers of June, the thanks of the people, and the joy of movement? Perhaps this could be a community project where persons walk from one church to another to view a visual floral display, give thanks to God and proclaim our faith dramatically to the community.

There are more elaborate types of outdoor parades your church might like to investigate this summer.

There could be a circus parade of Noah's Ark. There could be tableau scenes from the Bible arranged on flatbed trucks and driven through the community (remember to get a parade permit).

In the midst of the church's pomp and pageantry and carefully rehearsed ceremonies these parades allow for joyful spontaneity and inclusiveness. All join in, from the most important to the humblest person — from your oldest member to your playful children.

When we think of parades we think of clowns and these characters have moved into our churches in recent years exemplifying Paul's statement, "I am a fool for Christ."

Clowns could be introduced in these spontaneous parades. Their major job could be to check the children by leading them in the right direction — by taking their hands and parading with them — by adjusting their clothing or lifting their spirits. What makes us laugh? Slapstick of course appeals to all ages but has a very special appeal to the young who like all forms of physical humor.

You might want to use clowns in your worship service and summer is a good time to begin.

A leader might introduce clowns with something like this:

Many times our church services help us consider serious and solemn subjects. Many times our church services have periods of silence where we sit and listen for God's word. Many times we use our best formal manners to show our great respect for God. But our God is the God of all creation. He has given us many wonderful gifts and one of these is laughter. It seems that children have an especially abundant supply of this gift. Children seem to understand better than we adults, that work, though necessary and good, is not the end of life. God puts us in his world to sometimes just laugh and enjoy. Sometimes God says to us "Wait a minute! This is not a grim, dull, motionless world. I have created a world of hope and joy, a world in which the unexpected can happen, a world of laughter. There are many skits by clowns appropriate for an informal worship service.

An excellent resource for skits and information to help you in clown ministry activities is The Clown Ministry Handbook by Janet Litherland, published by Contemporary Drama Service.

A church group interested in exploring the possibilities of clown ministry will find this book invaluable. The author Janet Litherland says:

> "A clown is asexual, interracial, and ageless. He can touch at one time all ages, all intellects, all strata of society, the living, and the dying. Instant communication. He encompasses all human emotion and expresses it in a big, exaggerated way, showing his beloved audience that they might 'let it all out,' too, and feel better for it. In this way, he is a healer. By disclosing his own weakness, he risks himself, knowing not whether he will be praised or plagued, cheered, or heckled. He is vulnerable to his audience and he can be trusted."

In addition this is a very practical book. Basic instructions are included for clown make-up, for wardrobe and props. Where clown ministry can take place is discussed and a number of skits and gags are also included. A bibliography directing you where to find additional help is at the back of the book.

Clowns can also be used to bring your congregation to the period of prayer.

"**Leader:** One of the characters that we associate with laughter is a clown. When we laugh at clowns we are really laughing at ourselves and that is good. We shouldn't always take ourselves so seriously. We are going to use clowns today to help us focus our prayer time.

There are three kinds of clowns. The first which we will discuss are whiteface clowns. *(One or more clowns enter in whiteface, wearing sad expressions, torn clothes.)*

These poor clowns always look as if they are about to cry. Nothing they do seems to work out. Everything is always going wrong for them. *(Clowns do a few simple routines. For example, one picks up a chair and it falls to pieces. He finally sits down and gets stuck in the seat.)*

Unison Prayer: Heavenly Father, we are all sad-faced clowns at times. Help us to see the funny side when everything goes wrong and help us never to forget that your world is a world of hope and joy. Amen.

Leader: There are also august (pronounced "ow-ghoost") clowns.

(These clowns enter. They are the slapstick clowns. They wear pants that fall down, noses that light up and huge shoes they trip over. These clowns do a few routines.)

Leader: We laugh at these clowns because what happens to them is so unexpected.

Unison Prayer: Heavenly Father, help us always to be aware that we live in a world where the unexpected can happen. Keep us open to the joy this belief brings. Amen."*

Leader: And there are acrobat clowns. *(These clowns enter. They turn tumblesaults, cartwheels, ride unicycles and walk on stilts. They perform for the congregation.)*

Unison Prayer: Heavenly Father, these clowns, too, remind us that life is full of new possibilities, new ways of doing things. Keep us open to new awareness you have planned for us in this world of surprise and delight. Amen.

Following this the clowns lead the congregation to the church lawn where persons are waiting with helium balloons for each member of the congregation, or at least for all the children. On a signal from a clown these balloons are released and sail forth joyfully into the community.

Another way to take drama into the community in the context of lightheartedness and gaiety is to have your youth group or adults from your drama group who have a playful quality prepare a "Hotch-Potch" play and present it to community child care centers.

A "Hotch-Potch" play is a form of children's theatre where adults do the acting for children but the setting is so informal (usually the children surround the stage as in theatre-in-the-round) that the audience becomes participants, the children become a part of the action and even, in some cases, determine the direction of the play. Chase scenes dash into the audience. Hide and seek takes place among the chairs. Children cry out instructions to the actors: "Watch Out!", "Hurry!", "Come On!".

* From Let's Celebrate Laughter, copyright 1979 C.S.S. Publishing Company, Lima, Ohio Used with permission.

The following is an excerpt from a "Hotch-Potch" play; The King's Bad Moods by Judy Gattis Smith, published by Contemporary Drama Service.

THE KING'S BAD MOODS

KING SAUL: *(Muttering to himself)* So many people like David better than they do me. They think he is a greater warrior than I am. I will not stand for that! After all I am the King. No one can take my place. I will have to <u>kill</u> him.

JONATHAN: *(To children)* Oh no, my father can't mean that! He wouldn't <u>kill</u> David.

KING SAUL: I'll ask David to play for me again and while he is singing I'll throw this spear at him. I must get rid of him. *(Saul calls for his soldier)* Send for my servant, David. Tell him I want him to play for me again.

JONATHAN: *(Facing children)* No, no this is terrible. We must warn David. If he comes by you warn him that the King is going to kill him. *(Sits again biting fingernails, looking worried.)*
(David enters. If children warn him David ad libs with them: "Really?" "Thank you for the warning." "I'll be careful." If they don't warn him Jonathan warns him. David comes to the stage.)

JONATHAN: *(contd) (To children)* We forgot to tell him about the spear. If you see the king raise his spear warn David to duck. It's his only chance!

KING SAUL: Ah, yes David. Will you sing for me again? I seem to have one of my old headaches coming on.

DAVID: Of course. *(David begins to sing. Saul walks behind him and raises his spear. Children from audience cry, "Duck". David ducks to one side. Spear goes into audience.) (To children)* Thank you. You saved my life.
(Saul rushes to retrieve his spear. He raises it again. David is picking up his harp and dusting it off. He does not notice Saul. The children warn David again. Again he ducks and Saul's spear goes into the audience on the other side.) .

(Jonathan leads children in saying: "Run, David, Run")
(David runs into audience. He hides among the children.
Saul comes after him after again retrieving his spear.
There is hide and seek between Saul and David in the
audience for a while. This will have to be played freely
using the children's responses. Saul can ask, "Where is
he? Have you seen him?" of the children. David can
ask, "Will you hide me? Where can I go?" Finally they
both run out of the room.)

There are numerous children's summer theatres (usually outdoors) that have plays of this type in the summer but a Hotch-Potch play uses a Bible story as its basis. And though the actors "play with the script" they remain true to the central Bible message. Each one-act play in the Hotch-Potch series uses only three or four characters. Usually one carload so it is easy to take this into the community.

Plays of this type are so spontaneous and simple to develop that it is possible for a group of youth and adults (with some drama experience) to meet together on Monday, create their own one-act scenario, prepare costumes and props and be ready to give the play on Friday. I have followed this format on several occasions at summer youth camps.

Taking drama into the community makes the community aware of the church. Let's look now at the other side of the coin. How can we make the church aware of the community? Let's look at drama as an agent of social concerns.

Drama raises awareness of the congregation in a powerful way. Hearing about the death of 1,000 people leaves us untouched but seeing, dramatically portrayed, the death of one child reaches us deeply.

For centuries drama has been used to sensitize persons to problems, challenges and answers in our community. Drama has a special voice for illuminating the problems Christians face, for helping us make ethical decisions in the light of the Christian faith.

A strong teaching method would be to take a group of adults (perhaps an Adult Class) to a community play which deals with great human themes. Shakespeare or a Greek drama is a logical choice but do not rule out contemporary plays.

What should an adult church group attending such a drama together look for? Some things to keep in mind are:

1. Playwrights do not expect to have a system of thought represented in each of their scripts. If they did their works would be only dramatized dictums of philosophy or theology.

2. Also, they do not try to have their characters totally consistent in their thinking. If the latter were true, the drama would not portray true human nature.

3. Not everything is explained. If so the play does not have mystery and depth that characterize great literary expression.

4. Look at the characters: Who are they? What are their main goals? How and why do they respond to each other?

5. Look at the dialogue.

Following the play the group would meet at someone's home to discuss the impact of the production.

Are there other ways that drama can be used in social concerns?

1. Drama could be used to help Americanize foreign-born children and adults. American customs, lore and history would be more easily grasped through drama than probably any other means.

2. There is a new awareness in our churches of the contributions of the handicapped. This could be highlighted through drama.

3. Persons with special problems, such as the mentally retarded, become more real to us through drama. We view them with compassion.

4. Benefits of courtesy and cooperation could be presented to the socially handicapped through humorous drama. This is a much more pleasant way of correction.

5. The Bible stories could be dramatically presented to children in settlement homes, migrant ministries, deprived neighborhoods. There is a new realization of the value of dramatic work in molding children's social values. These children could be helped to create their own settings and costumes for their own dramatic productions thereby helping them gain the self-assurance and confidence necessary to rise above one's environment.

6. A special Sunday could be observed in your church — "Ephphatha Sunday" — based on the passage from Isaiah 35:5, 6: "The ears of the deaf shall be unstopped. The tongue of the dumb shall sing." The title comes from the Aramaic word, "Ephphatha" which means "Be opened". The entire service could be used to bring to the congregation's attention the church's work among the deaf and dumb. There are numerous dramatic possibilities in sign language.

There is still another way that the drama group and the local church can minister to the community.

The church can serve as the base of operation for a community drama group. In this case the church would be the landlord. Either absentee or not, encouraging the use of their space by both religious and secular theatrical groups. The church of course could be an active part of this arrangement, serving as producer and promoter and producing plays in keeping with the concerns of the community — peace, social justice and faith renewal. The church's involvement could be an extension of how it views its ministry or the church could just provide space — just open its doors for artists to come and perform. It would be performing the role of the Innkeeper in the Good Samaritan.

This kind of service would necessitate a community where there is a high concentration of dramatic talent. It would arise in a viable creative community.

A possible direction this might take is a lunch-time arts program — a multi-faceted, art-oriented noonday program of drama, monologues, and other art media. Persons from the community could drop in on their own terms, draw their own conclusions and enter into dialogue with the arts. Persons could accept, reject or reflect upon their experiences.

Another possibility is the availability of the church's Fellowship Hall for rehearsals by community groups. In some communities finding a large rehearsal space is a problem.

This program might take the direction of housing regular community drama on an on-going basis with the church building a theatre or converting unused space to this purpose.

Whichever direction the church takes, the community (and not just that of the church goers) is the ultimate beneficiary of the creative force in their midst. The service the church provides in this case is to open their doors and spaces to the art community and to minister to their congregation in modern, relevant ways. The church, in these settings, may find the arts can be the most persuasive of their missionary activities.

JULY:

Accoutrements of Drama
Make-Up, Costumes, Scenery

July arrives and it's hot! Sidewalks sizzle, pavements glare, the street is an oven. Garden produce is mature and ripe, the days are long, dogs pant, dragonflies hover — even the shade is hot! And, the only creatures moving with energy are the little ants; or, perhaps, your Drama Group!

During these light-long days and long green weeks plan for Summer Enrichment Days for your children where they can investigate all the fun accoutrements of drama — experiment with make-up and disguises, create costumes wild and fantastic, paint backdrops that push the imagination to the limits, bring to life original puppets and use Bible stories to bring all of this into focus.

Long July afternoons can be times for this Summer Enrichment: Wonderful Wednesdays or Terrific Tuesdays or whatever day fits your situation. Invite all of your children, first grade through sixth grade and let the teenagers come too, serving as aids and extra hands.

Begin with puppets. Puppets are an enjoyable and enlightening method for children to communicate with each other. Puppets can be used in two ways: 1) as spontaneous, informal drama; and 2) in scripted puppet story/dramatizations.

For example: In situations involving moral decisions two students could give their views or take opposing views in a puppet act. Topics for this type of program might be: shoplifting, cheating on tests, keeping a promise, being a tattletale or other similar subjects dealing with childhood character development.

Young children can act out their feelings through puppets: sad times, happy times, times they were frightened, times of anxiety and worry.

In a more formal skit puppets can help visualize, recreate and reinforce a lesson or Bible story. Children can write and produce their own skit. Don't underestimate how creative your class can be. They might tape record the dialogue or tape background mood music. A narrator could simply tell a Bible story while the puppet cast presents the dialogue. You might wish to share the group's production with parent participation.

Let the imagination of the children have free rein. The purpose of puppetry is creative self-expression giving the child a chance to use his or her own imagination in interpreting things in his/her own way. The fun of puppets is that they can be anything their creator desires — people, animals, or wild figments of the imagination. Puppets help a child develop self-expression. Often a shy child will blossom when he gets behind the puppet stage.

What about some specifics to make your puppets more professional? There are three aspects of a puppet's character:

1. What does it look like
2. How does it move
3. How does it speak

There are many books on form, features, costumes, and color to give your puppets their distinct appearance.

Think about how you want your puppet to appear. Take time to give it a style, a special look.

A few hints on movements are:

1. Move only the puppet who is talking; the others should freeze.

2. Do not move the puppet on every word. Move only on the important words, actions, or reactions.

3. All movements should be clean and distinct; keep movements simple.

4. Find expressive movements that identify your puppet and repeat them.

5. Make movement without haste — no wiggling without purpose.

Voice characterization is important. It confirms the personality of the puppet's appearance. These are the most important considerations in giving voices to your puppets:

1. Keep speeches short. What the puppet does is more important than what he says.

2. Use a puppet voice, never use a human voice.

3. The voice should be as big or as small as the puppet's relative size. The voice should never overwhelm the puppet.

4. If there is more than one puppet in a play, the puppets should have contrasting voices: high and low, loud and soft, old and young.

5. Each puppet should have his own voice. It must be a constant voice so that he/she does not step out of character.

An example of using simple puppets to reinforce a Bible story follows:

"**Leader:** Today we are going to hear a Bible story. Our story takes place many years ago, in a family. The father of the family was named Isaac.

(Puppet appears, points to self, bows.)

The mother was named Rebekah.

(Puppet appears, points to self, bows.)

Isaac and Rebekah wanted a son very badly. They were overjoyed when they had not one son — but two — twin boys whom they named Jacob and Esau.

(Puppets appear, point to self, bow.)

Esau grew up to be an outdoors man, a skillful hunter and trapper. Jacob was quiet, preferring to stay indoors. The Bible says "Isaac loved Esau but Rebekah loved Jacob."

(Isaac puts arm around Esau, Rebekah puts arm around Jacob.) (Puppets go Offstage)

Finally Isaac grew very old. His eyesight dimmed until he could barely see.

(Isaac comes tottering Onstage)

He called his favorite son, Esau, to him.

(Waves hand toward body) (Esau appears)

Isaac told him that he was getting very old and the time had come for him to give to his son, all his lands and all his cattle and most important, his special blessing. But first, he said, take your bow and arrow and go and kill some game for me and cook it your special way for I do love your cooking.

(Esau nods in agreement and leaves) (Isaac leaves)

But, unknown to Isaac, Rebekah had overheard the conversation.

(Rebekah comes up, looks around.)

"It's not fair!" she thought. "Jacob is smarter. He should not just be left out in the cold. If Esau gets the special blessing Jacob will have nothing. And Esau likes hunting and the out-of-doors. He can always take care of himself. But what will happen to poor Jacob?"

Then she had an idea.

(Rubs hands together to express cunning)

She called Jacob and told him her plan.

(Jacob appears, puppets bend heads toward each other to suggest talking together.)

"While Esau is out hunting," she said, "I'll make some stew out of goat meat and you can take it in to him and he'll bless you instead of Esau."

(Rebekah brings up large, oversized dish.)

"Here it is, all simmering and bubbling just the way he likes it." But Jacob shook his head.

(Puppet rotates back and forth to express negative idea)

"I don't think this is going to work. Esau is hairy and I am not. What if he feels my hands and arms and figures out it is Jacob not Esau?"

Rebekah has another idea.

(Taps head lightly with one hand to express thinking)
(Rebekah pops below and brings up yarn. She puts it on Jacob.)

Rebekah took some of the skin from the goat and put it on Jacob's arms and neck. Then she dressed him in Esau's clothes.

(Drapes skin around him)

"Now, he'll never know the difference."

(Rebekah leaves)

So Jacob, dressed as Esau, took the food and went in to Isaac to be blessed.

(Jacob bows before Isaac)

"Here I am, Father. Give me your blessing."

(Isaac appears)

"You sound like Jacob." Isaac said, "Let me feel your arms."

(Puppet feels other puppet)

"Well, I guess you are Esau. I can't see very well, you know. Here is my blessing upon you."

(Places hand on Jacob's head, Jacob bows.)

"Now all that I have is yours."

(Isaac leaves)

Jacob and Rebekah were very happy. The blessing was Jacob's.

(Puppets express joy by clapping hands and dancing together)

After a while Esau returned.

(Puppet appears)

When he learned about the trick that had been played on him he let out an angry scream and he vowed to get even with Jacob.

(Esau waves arms in anger)

Poor Jacob was very frightened.

(Puppet trembles)

He was afraid Esau would murder him for what he had done. So, all alone, Jacob sneaked away from his home.

(Puppet turns and waves goodbye)

He walked and he ran, always afraid of being followed.

(Puppet moves up and down in a choppy manner while crossing stage to give illusion of running.)

His feet were bruised from the stones and his eyes ached from the sun and dust. Jacob realized he had done a wicked thing. Although he had his father's blessing he was alone, in a strange country with no mother and father and no brother.

(Puppet leaves)

What would have happened if there had been forgiveness in the family?

Isaac, come here.

(Puppet appears)

The story would have ended differently if you had forgiven Jacob for not being strong and manly like Esau and shared your inheritance with both of them.

(Puppet bows head to floor in shame)

Rebekah, come here.

(Puppet appears)

The story would have ended differently if you had forgiven Esau for not being as smart or as handsome as Jacob and if you had talked to Isaac about sharing his inheritance instead of trying to trick him.

(Puppet bows head to floor)

Jacob and Esau, come here.

(Puppets appear)

You needed to learn how to live in a family, too. Living in a family means not only doing things for others but trying to understand each other and then accepting what we cannot understand without blame. All the characters in this story suffered because they had not acted in a loving manner."*

(Puppets leave)

Another area for Summer Enrichment is to let your students explore the world of make-up. Buy a make-up kit at any store that sells theatrical materials or send to Contemporary Drama Service for a Ben Nye Make-up Kit ($23.95 plus shipping).

Theatercraft For Church and School by Louise Ulmer, published by Contemporary Drama Service, is an excellent resource to help you. In the chapter on Make-up the author suggests: "Ask ladies to clean out their make-up boxes and give you what they don't want. You may not

---

* From A Better Way: A Liturgy For Children, Copyright 1979, C.S.S. Publishing Company, Inc., Lima, Ohio. Used with permission.

have to buy a thing. Two articles are absolutely indispensable — dark eyebrow pencil and red lipstick.''

Use a room with mirror space. Ideally the setting would allow students to be seated in front for a table with a mirror directly in front of them. Look around your church. There is usually a mirror in the Choir Room and in the Bride's Room (or Parlor) that you could borrow and turn horizontally. Pre-school Sunday School rooms sometimes have a standing mirror in their dress-up corner.

Have an artist from your congregation draw facial expressions on paper plates using simple lines to suggest worry, surprise, and other basic emotions. Tape these paper plates on the walls to give your students inspiration. Again, the book Theatercraft For Church and School gives illustrations and instructions for such effects as wrinkles, circles, frown lines, etc.

Next, read or tell a Bible story to the group using a character with a distinct visual image. Then let the students go to work creating this character on their own face by use of theatre make-up.

A variation is to let one student make-up another and then reverse.

Some suggestions for characters are:

1. The oldest man in the Bible. Do you need beards? Whitening powder for the hair? (Read Genesis 5)

2. Wild man from the land of the Gadarenes before he was healed by Jesus. Imaginations can go wild here. (Luke 8:24-40)

3. What about Jezebel? How would her beauty be different from Esther? Both were noted for their beauty. How could facial make-up show the difference? (Book of Esther and I Kings 21 for Jezebel)

4. Look at the disciples. How would they depict Judas? (Subtle evil?) Thomas? (Doubting).

5. The rich young ruler. How could pride be depicted in facial make-up?

To further enhance the face you might try the following simple additions:

A curly beard could be created by folding a piece of 9" x 12" construction paper in half. Fringe along the open side almost to the fold. Curl the fringe by pulling it over the sharp edge of a scissors blade. Add mustache.

Make the mustache by folding construction paper in half. Draw a half of any style mustache shape along the fold. Cut out the shape and open the paper. Tape to upper lip.

For a more professional effect use the instructions for beards in Theatercraft For Church and School.

Goggle eyes could be created by using an egg carton. Cut away two adjoining cup sections. Cut holes for eyes in bottom of each cup. Tape the eyes to the head.

A final note in the make-up chapter of Theatercraft For Church and School gives suggestions for the care and storage of your make-up.

All age levels could profit from this exercise. Teenagers and adults might receive enlightenment. Children respond with open fun.

The group might be so inspired by their own handiwork that they would want to write an original skit using all these characters and others in a "Parade of Bible Faces" or "What our Faces tell Us about Ourselves".

Another drama activity that can make interesting Summer Enrichment is a scenery making workshop.

James Hull Miller's book Self Supporting Scenery, published by Contemporary Drama Service, is a detailed workbook of stagecraft for free-standing scenery, including scene design, scene painting, lighting. It is a how-to-do-it book covering tools, materials, designs and crafts.

The author states, "A scene design is a scheme for making scenery which tells an audience something important about a play's environment. It may be a sketch, a model, a diagram or even an idea. The design itself need not have any inherent artistic value. It is given significance only when the scenery created from it proves successful in productions."

The Bible is full of strange and wonderful stories that inspire exciting set design. Read these stories with the students. Then, giving imagination free rein create a wide variety of designs. Use the full spectrum of colors and then create some of your own colors. Be literal — be symbolic — be highly interpretive. Think in new ways — visualize in your mind. Let your imagination soar!

Then actually build a set using the help of Mr. Miller's book.

It could be used as a backdrop for an original storytelling or as an inspiring design in your Drama or Church School room.

Some Biblical stories that suggest creative designs are: Tower of Babel, Jonah and the Whale, Ezekiel and the Valley of the Dry Bones, Daniel and the Mysterious Handwriting on the Wall, Moses and the Burning Bush, Daniel in the Fiery Furnace, Deborah and the 900 chariots, The Garden of Eden, Jacob and the Ladder of Angels, Moses crossing the Red Sea, and Joshua and the Walls of Jericho.

Making costumes can be a creative experience for long July days. Remember, costumes are seen from a distance so the "effect" is what we are trying to create.

A whole character can be built under a hat or on a pair of boots. Costumes in theatre must reflect the character simply and clearly and this can be done in partial costume.

A basic sack costume that requires no sewing, is simple to make and offers a variety of possibilities for use follows.

BASIC SACK COSTUME: Measure a length of cloth as wide as the distance from the elbow to elbow with arms extended and twice as long as the distance from neck to knees.

Fold material in half — wrong side out. Staple the sides together, leaving holes for the arms. Cut two holes for the legs.

Turn the sack right side out. Make slits at intervals near the top and thread a ribbon or string through the slits.

Have a child step into the sack. If desired the sack can be stuffed with shredded or crumpled newspaper until it is round and full.

Sandwich boards are quick, effective costumes. All you need are two large pieces of cardboard which can be decorated, painted or shaped in any way you wish.

Pleated paper offers possibilities for costumes. Folded in accordion pleats it is extremely versatile. Use it to make a collar, wings, head-dress or tails.

Ordinary material such as paper bags and cardboard boxes become imaginative costumes. Use grocery boxes big enough for children to climb into. Children paint torsos on the boxes.

Collect material, ends of bolts or used sheets, to make a basic toga costume. Measure the child, fold the material in half. Cut a hole for the head in the center of the fold. Pull it together with a sash and there you are. Bits of material also make excellent headdresses.

Tie-dying a large oversized T-shirt is a fun way to create a costume that gives the effect of clothing worn in Jesus' day.

Chapter 4, "Costumes and Props" of Theatercraft For Church and School gives suggestions for variations of the basic sack dress. In addition you will find: What the well-dressed shepherd is wearing, Greek and Roman high fashion, Egyptian headdress and a Roman Soldier's armor.

One of the most enjoyable things about drama is that it uses so many artistic skills. Not only those in front of the audience are important but a host behind stage — making sets, creating make-up, designing costumes. Hopefully this month's activities will demonstrate this to all participants.

AUGUST:

Imagination & Play as Drama

It's August!

Summer is ending. Trees seem to be bored with being green and are anxious for their new Fall outfits. Insects are playing their last loud concerts before packing up their instruments for another year. Everything seems to shimmer with gold this month — gold marigolds, ripe pears, swallowtail butterflies, tasseled corn and big gold moons.

In the twilights of these long summer days there are hours for fantasy and fun.

Your drama group has had a long, busy year. In this month tempers and temperatures may compete. Let's enjoy it with relaxation and play. It is no coincidence that the word for the main activity of childhood is the same as the word for what is done in theatre. Children play games and playwrights write plays. Performers were called "players" long before they were called actors. The place of performance was called a "playhouse" before it was called a theatre.

In a sense drama has two origins. One in the history of mankind and one in the childhood of each person.

If you look closely at the play of children there is drama.

Dramatic actions are used: handkerchief is dropped, the tag is made, home is touched. These are clean-cut dramatic actions.

Children's love of chant and repetitive catch phrases in their games echoes drama.

Children create a fantasy world with toys. What most often holds the fascination of a child is not the objective toy but the potential for make believe that the toy engenders.

Dramatic play for children brings serious issues of life to a form in which the child can not only learn to cope but to enjoy coping.

The sports activities that children love also contain drama. Heroic roles abound. Goals get scored and runs made. The possibility of being a hero is always present. There is much emotional expression in the activity of children.

In the broadest sense there are many types of techniques for informal drama. One of these is surely creative play.

Wherever there is drama there should be the sense of fun and games.

We know that children have always played. In Zechariah 8:5 it speaks of "boys and girls playing in the streets." Following are five games from Bible stories reprinted from the book, Games From Bible Lands & Times* that children will enjoy playing.

It is well to remember that children make poor spectators while games are being played unless the activities are fairly fast moving, interesting or amusing. Those who are forced to remain inactive throughout a game should, whenever possible, be given the chance to play the same game later on.

Game 1: Locust

"The locust have no king, yet they go forth in bands."
(Proverbs 30:27)

These troublesome insects which raided and stripped the grain fields in Biblical times were kept out of the field by every possible means. Look in a Bible storybook for pictures of locust or at least a grain field.

A 32-foot square is plainly marked on the ground. Inside it a 20-foot square is marked and in the middle is a 10-inch paper plate stapled to the ground.
All outside the big square are locust. Guarding the inner square are guards to keep the locust out of the fields. (See drawing, next page.)

---

* Reprinted from Games From Bible Lands & Times by Allan MacFarlan, Copyright 1965.
  By permission of New Century Publishers, Inc., Piscataway, N.J. 08854.

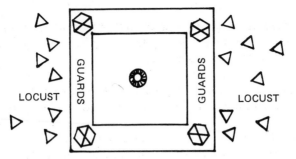

When the leader says "GO" the locust try to slip past the guards, enter field, touch "grain" without being tagged by a guard. Any locust who succeeds in doing this wins 5 points and can go back outside the square without being touched by the guards.

Any guard who tags a locust is given 5 points and the locust is out of the game. No guard may touch a locust until he enters the big square.

Who will win, the locust or the guards?

Game 2: Tambourine Tap

"They take the timbrel and harp and rejoice." (Job 21:12)

Look at pictures of musical instruments in the Bible. Learn the Bible verse.

The biblical name for a tambourine-type of musical instrument was the timbrel or tabret.

A player is blindfolded and given a tambourine. This player sits in the middle of a circle 20-feet in diameter while four other players, not blindfolded, stand just outside the circle. One player on each of the four sides of the circle. The object of the game is for these four players to steal up, one at a time, and try to tap the tambourine before they are tagged by the player holding the tambourine.

The leader points to any one of the four players as a signal that he should start his silent advance and then the player may approach from any side he wishes.

Game 3: Lot's Wife

"But his wife looked back from behind him and she became a pillar of salt." (Genesis 19:26)

Players line up three feet apart in a straight line. A player, chosen as Spotter, stands thirty feet in front of the other players with his/her back to them. The Spotter calls "ready" and begins to count up to six aloud. On "one" the other players begin to advance, not faster than a walk. They must be ready to stop as soon as the Spotter says "six". The Spotter swings around quickly and any player seen moving a foot or body is called Lot's wife and must stand still exactly at that spot for the rest of the game. Being spotted has turned the player into a pillar of salt.

The Spotter continues. The player passing the Spotter wins and becomes the Spotter.

Game 4: Crocodile and Fish

Recall with the children the times when the People of Israel were slaves in the land of Egypt.

You need a slide to play this game. Choose a crocodile. He or she will stand one big step in front of the slide.

When the Fish come down the slide, the Crocodile tries to catch them. But he cannot move his feet from the spot where he is standing.

The fish come down the slide. They cannot slow down towards the end. But they try not to land in the arms of the Crocodile.

The first fish the Crocodile catches becomes the next Crocodile.

Each player is on his own and all his efforts are directed toward keeping out of the Crocodile's grasp. Children of the Nile endeavored to do so in Biblical times but, in their case, it was not a game.

Game 5: Turtle Tag

One player is the Seagull. Everyone else is a Turtle. The Seagull chases the Turtles and tries to tag them. As soon as the Seagull comes close enough the Turtles lie on their backs with hands and legs in the air. This is the only way the Turtles are safe.

If all the Turtles are lying down the Seagull takes three giant steps away from the nearest one and counts aloud to ten.

Whoever doesn't get up and run away in time gets tagged. That person becomes the next Seagull.

Children in Biblical times, just as today, liked to mimic the motions of animals.

Examination of child play reveals one fact above all others and that is the power of the child's dramatic imagination. It can transform reality of the environment and endow everyday objects with fantastic qualities.

One method of teaching drama to adults utilizes this idea of drama as play. The term "theatre games" has meaning to many drama students. It is another term for improvisational drama where original ideas, characters and story lines evolve "on-the-spot" from the participant's own imaginations. Spontaneity is the key word.

For example, pantomime games might be used:

1.   Using a broom. Recreating actions without the broom.

2.   Tug-of-war with actual rope. Then remove the rope and recreate. Feel the rope!

3.   Play ball with imaginary balls of varying weights and sizes. Know where the ball is.

4.   Students could take turns pantomiming all sorts of sounds; a drip, a splash, a boom, a crack, a zoom, a slam, a pop, etc.

5.   Each player could be assigned a game or sport. Others guess what the game or sport is. Some examples: skating, bird-watching, football, baseball, croquet, etc.

This idea of using game structure as a basis for theatre training was developed by Viola Spolin * as a means of freeing amateurs from mechanical, stilted stage behavior.

It can be used in a local church setting to enrich persons; to make them more sensitive, creative and aware. It may be used as a warm-up exercise before beginning work on any dramatic presentation. Through drama we stir up the creative gifts within us.

* Northwestern University Press

Games that sensitize us are good. Those who have been in formal plays know that mashed potatoes are served as ice cream and stone walls are made of canvas. An actor, through his sensory equipment, must make real for an audience what is not real. Not only actors, but any person is more alive and vital and certainly more creative when he is aware of his senses.

Begin by listening. Sit quietly for one minute and listen to the sounds of your immediate environment. What do you hear?

Use the sense of touch by playing an "identifying objects" game.

Use sense of sight by placing a dozen or more objects on a tray. Give the students fifteen seconds to look. Then cover the tray. How many objects can they remember?

Move from these games to creating little scenes. Have an imaginary setting of a corner bus stop. Let each student choose a character to come and wait on the bus. Students decide on age and action.

Set a scene from the Bible. Each student could be a character along the Via Dolorosa as Jesus comes by dragging his cross. Show age and reaction of your character.

Be one of the children of Israel as you approach the Red Sea with Moses. What emotions will you portray?

As Vivian Smith says, "Surely the ability to create and the ability to play are two of the greatest gifts God gave to man. The use of informal drama invites us to participate in a blend of these two processes and to work and share with others as we do so."

August is also a good month to look at storytelling. Drama tells a story. It does more than tell a story but telling a story is its prime function.

In the early days of Israel, God's actions were sung and told in the marketplace by Psalmists and storytellers. They were ancient forerunners of the art of drama.

In this month of campfires and evenings at the beach what are some helps for the storyteller?

First, of course, is the choosing of the right story for the right setting.

A number of kits are available from Contemporary Drama Service with stories ready for the telling. There is a collection of Indian Stories. These would certainly be appropriate for August campfires and as a quiet respite for hikes or overnight camping.

Some of the best stories for campfires are found in the Bible.

There is just something about a "told" story that grabs our interest in a way no other form of communication can. With children on long vacation trips the magic words seem to be, "Let me tell you a story". Have you ever noticed how a congregation perks up when a minister moves into a story during his sermon? Teachers testify to the magic of a story when nothing else seems to work in a classroom.

To tell a story well is a dramatic talent that can be developed with practice. Perhaps members of your drama group would like to share their time and talents in telling and listening as every member sharpens his or her own skills.

Each of the story kits from Contemporary Drama Service contains "Suggestions for the Storyteller":

"Don't think you're ready once you've mastered the story mechanics. It's what you do after this that separates the really good storyteller from the mediocre. Make the story yours. Catch its mood and adapt it to your individual personality and talents. Figure how you can tell it best. The words. The gestures. The pacing. Experiment, telling the high points of the story aloud. Storytelling is not a conventional dramatization but a personal communication."

If you are telling your story out-of-doors be sure you are in a setting where you can be heard. Speaking against even a summer breeze requires lung power.

C.G. Jung describes how difficult it was for him to humble himself and play the imagination games of a child and the value of that experience. Just as children need to learn to think logically, adults need to rediscover the magical reality of the imagination. We must always strive to keep in touch with the child within us.

It might be helpful on occasion to write down some incident you remember from your childhood. In reflective moments see how far back you can go in your childhood memories. Try to recapture the feelings of childhood.

Play, drama and imagination can lead us to God.

POSTSCRIPT

Our drama year comes to an end. Looking to the seasons we have tried
to discover, as Saint Francis says in *The Canticle to Brother Sun:*

> "All the weather's moods
> By which you cherish all that you have made."

The freshness of Spring, the ripe maturity of Summer, the haunting
sadness of Autumn, the starkness of Winter — all speak, in a unique
way to our imaginations. All find their particular expression in some
form of drama.

In the same way, the Liturgical Year supports us and directs us into a
deeper experience of life made known through Christ.

Each of the seasons has action, symbols and words that express the
church's story which has developed down through the centuries. These
too find expression through drama.

We move to a level of human understanding that is nonverbal and non-
rational and is conveyed by symbolic forms and actions.

These dramatic actions open up our imaginations. Imagination — that
marvelous gift of God that came so spontaneously to us as children
but which for our adult years we have been trained to disregard, even
fear.

Your drama group might gather to evaluate the year. Wherever there
is drama there is fun and excitement. Laugh together over the many
joyful mistakes and catastrophes typical of drama production. Remember that high point that was reached. Recall the good feeling following
a production. Try to recapture the "butterflies of excitement" before
going Onstage.

In a somber moment someone might ask: Why did we put so much
effort and energy into this particular group in the church? Would our
time not be better spent doing good deeds — helping the needy?
Should we feel guilty about playing? About having so much fun?

Then remember the purpose of religious drama which is the awaken-
ing of the imagination — the receiving of the many-faceted gifts of
God that certainly enrich the lives of others.

About the Author

Judy Gattis Smith is nationally heralded as a Christian drama writer for children. She has authored five books for leading publishers in the field. Her materials make Sunday school teachers everywhere feel as if she's been in their shoes for years, and knows just how to keep super-active children interested.

All her materials provide ways to teach children the basic truths of the Bible without their feeling as if it's all "boring" study. In this book, she provides enough ideas that your kids can become creative on their own.

For several years, she has written curriculum material for the United Methodist Church. She is active as director of Christian ministries and education at the Williamsburg United Methodist Church in Williamsburg, Virginia, where her husband David is senior pastor.